AUSTRIAN ACADEMY OF SCIENCES
SAPIENZA UNIVERSITY OF ROME

XI Coffee Break Conference

ARRANGED MARRIAGES BETWEEN DISCIPLINES

ROME, 10–11 DECEMBER 2021
VIENNA, 16–17 DECEMBER 2021

.

Book of abstracts

Edited by A. Keidan

COFFEE BREAK PROJECT
ROME, VIENNA
2021

ISBN 978-1-7947-4789-0

XI Coffee Break Conference: Arranged Marriages between Disciplines. Rome, 10–11 December 2021; Vienna, 16–17 December 2021 / ed. by Artemij Keidan

Cover image: Qutb Minar, Delhi; photograph by A. Keidan

Published by Coffee Break Project

Visit https://asiaticacoffeebreak.wordpress.com

Summary

A Humanities' love triangle:
Anthropology, Literature, and Gender Studies

Conveners: Marco Lauri and Marta Scaglioni

The academic reading of literary texts has benefited significantly from anthropological insights and perspectives, while anthropologists, also, have come to integrate textual literary analysis to the arsenal of their methods and source material. It has been well-observed that themes and concerns of these two disciplines widely overlap, while their perspectives differ before their subjects of inquiry. However, understanding of identities and social roles, in particular, can and should be enriched by a combination of these disciplinary approaches. It is the point we feel where gender identities and gender roles also become relevant. It is known that gender identities and gender roles are well-studied in Anthropology and Literature, and Gender Studies have often tended toward either a historical or literary/textual approach to make weaker and silenced historical voices heard.

Taking into consideration all above-mentioned, our panel intends to put together these different but intertwined disciplinary approaches to shed light on various declinations of identity in the Muslim world, showing some of the complex interplays that emerge at the intersections of gender, race, ethnicity, class and nationality.

Martina Biondi
Gender relations and political resistance in Moroccan prison narratives

ABSTRACT

During the first part of the so-called "Moroccan Years of Lead" (1965–1999), Hassan II's regime harshly repressed Left-wing and Marxist-Leninist militants (Vermeren 2012). In this context, there were numerous women who underwent arbitrary detentions, tortures, and deaths (Saoudi 2004). Some of them have testified about their carceral experience in memories written either inside or outside prison. This paper explores the themes of gendered violence, political resistance, and corporeal memory as shaped in *Sīrat al-Ramād* ("Biography of Ash", 2000) by Khadija Marwazi, in Fatna El Bouih's *Ḥadīth al-ʿAtama* ("Tale from the Dark", 2001), and in Saida Manebhi's *Poèmes, lettres, écrits de prison* (1978).

The paper analyses political coercion and physical violence inflicted to female prisoners, as well as the strategies of negotiation and collective female "agency" within prison. It will provide a critical reading of the memoirs by identifying a trajectory from a gendered inflicted suffering (abuses and tortures) to an agentive self-inflicted pain (hunger strike), emphasizing the weaponization of women's bodies (Bargu 2014). As Saida Menebhi died because of the hunger strike, Fatna El Bouih's and Khadija Marwazi's "embodied memory" of the political violence emerges in the early 2000s. In this sense, gendered memoirs challenge Moroccan national history as a male-dominated narrative, proving, at the same time, a problematic picture of female engagement within the revolutionary groups.

REFERENCES

Bargu, B. 2014. *Starve and Immolate. The Politics of Human Weapons*. New York: Columbia University Press.

Bouih (al-), F. 2001. *Hadith al-ʿAtama*. Casablanca: Le Fennec, 2001.

Marwazi, Kh. 2000. *Sirat al-Ramad*. Casablanca: Afriqiya al-Sharq, 2000.

Menebhi, S. 1978. *Poèmes, lettres, écrits de prison*. Parigi: Comité de lutte contre la répression au Maroc.

Vermeren, P. 2012. *Histoire du Maroc depuis l'indépendance*. Parigi: La Découverte, 2012.

Saoudi, N.-E. 2004. "Il Marocco degli anni di piombo", in E. Bartuli (ed.). *Sole Nero: anni di piombo in Marocco*, 261–89. Messina: Mesogea.

Marco Lauri
Gender roles and social expectations
in the *One Thousand and One Nights*

ABSTRACT

The *One Thousand and One Nights* have been long recognised, among other things, as a trove of insights about the views on sexuality and gender roles in the Medieval Muslim world (Malti-Douglas 1991). The *Nights* have a complex compositional history and a hybrid genre positioning. This allows their reading not just as a literary text reflecting specific authorial views, but also as a document of social ideals and expectations, specifically regarding identities, gender relationships and gender roles. In this discussion, I will show how, in some of the stories of the collection, the views of gender roles and related social expectations expressed or suggested do put into question the accepted social norms.

This challenge was, however, formulated in ways that fit squarely into pre-existing normative tradition, both literary and cultural at large. This seems to be the case for the story "Ali Shar and Zumurrud", on which I will focus, comparing its similarities and differences in plot and its ideological underpinnings with the similar story of Maryam the Girdle-girl. This reading, that deploys anthropological, literary and historical methods to examine the texts, will end with the suggestion of a plausible socio-cultural environment for the composition of the story in the mid Mamluk period.

REFERENCES

Malti-Douglas, F. 1991. *Woman's body, woman's word: gender and discourse in Arabo-Islamic writing.* Princeton: Princeton University Press.

Neslihan Demirkol
Queering Turkish identity in *On the road to Baghdad*

ABSTRACT

Let me start with a question: how do we decide if a literary piece is a part of national literature or not? Based on the ethnic identity of the author or the language of the book? How do we answer this question for the Turkish-American author and translator Güneli Gün's *On the Road to Baghdad* (1991), the story of a 16th-century figure, Hürü, a fictional character mostly inspired by "the heroine figure of Turkish exemplary folk tales", which was first published in English, then translated into Turkish? If we say that it is not a part of Turkish literature because it is not initially published in Turkish, how can we explain the curious case of Halide Edip Adıvar's *The Clown and His Daughter*? The novel was first published in English (1935), then "in Turkish" (not "translated into Turkish"), received the literary awards by CHP, the founding party of Turkish Republic, and became one of the most important works of modern Turkish literary canon.

It is evident that the attempt to define a literary work with reference to national borders poses many challenges. However, Güneli Gün's "picaresque novel of magical adventures borrowed and stolen from the *One Thousand and One Nights*", where Hürü starts her journey from Istanbul to Baghdad in the 16th century but ends up travelling back in time to 8th century and finding herself at Abbasid Baghdad, also provides a queer representation of its heroine. Described as "bicultural" by Gönül Pultar, the novel presents us Hürü and Shahrazad as the embodiments of their ethnic cultures in binary opposition, Turkish/Central Asian-originated heroine vs Middle Eastern anti-heroine.

The two heroines display traces of how the Turkish identity constructs itself as opposed to Arabic identity through woman body. In other words, the ideal Turkish female character Hürü is attributed a fluid gender identity, which keeps changing through the narrative, while the representative of Middle Eastern Ar-

abic culture, Shahrazad, has a fixed gender role and identity with all characteristics of femininity. The question to be answered is that how and why queering
a female protagonist contributes to Turkish identity narrative in this novel.

REFERENCES
Adıvar, H. E. 193. *The Clown and His Daughter.* London: Allen & Unwin.
Gün, G. 1991. *On the Road to Baghdad A Picaresque Novel of Magical Adventures,
    Begged, Borrowed, and Stolen from the Thousand and One Nights.* London:
    Virago.

Marta Scaglioni
Care issues among the Egyptian diaspora in Milan between gender and ethnicity

ABSTRACT

The COVID-19 pandemic and the consequent socio-economic slowdown have provided a privileged standpoint to observe care relations and their transformations. This presentation analyzes ideas of care and mutualism through a multi-disciplinary angle, adopting an ethnographic approach to inquire the transformations occurring within the Egyptian diaspora in Milan.

In Spring 2020, Milan and its region, Lombardy, were hit very hard by the SARS COVID-19 pandemic. The "Lombardian model of welfare," marked by a «homegrown variety of neoliberalism suffused with elements of conservative Catholic social doctrine» (Muelenbach 2012: 15) struggled to cope with the spread of the virus and with the consequent socio-economic crisis, which took a heavy toll on migrants.

As a reaction, the Egyptian community in Milan has organized charity associations providing essential aid targeting all people in need, regardless of their faith. Currently, Egyptian women, whose employment rate is traditionally very low, play an important role in buying, stocking, and distributing goods. Their activity allows them to take a set of embodied practices connected to care (Aulino 2016) from the private to the public sphere.

This paper inquires the renegotiation and transformation of gender and generational relations within the diasporic Egyptian community in Milan, keeping an eye at the Islamic notion of *zakat* 'almsgiving'.

REFERENCES

Aulino, F. 2016. "Rituals of care for the elderly in northern Thailand. Merit, morality, and the everyday of long-term care", *American Ethnologist* 43.1: 91–101.
Muelenbach, A. 2012. *The Moral Neoliberal: Welfare and Citizenship in Italy*. Chicago and London: The University of Chicago Press.

Conceptuality in Perceptual Knowledge

Convener: Marco Ferrante

Epistemology is probably the most advanced branch of philosophy in premodern South Asia. The variety and the subtlety of the topics Indian theorists touched upon in their works is impressing and still very much relevant to the contemporary epistemological debate. The problems these intellectuals reflected upon are often similar to those that preoccupy Euro-American thinkers (the nature of truth and error, the mechanism by which one acquires knowledge etc.), but sometimes differ. Among the latter cases, one finds the question this panel focusses on, that is, the issue whether perceptual knowledge is a "purely perceptual" affair, or it entails some kind of conceptualisation.

Broadly speaking, a conceptualised cognition is a determ inate form of knowledge that implies the presence of language and meanings. Almost all Indian philosophical traditions shared the notion that direct perception is the most reliable means to acquire knowledge. Nevertheless, when they come to define it, differences start to emerge.

The most relevant one regards precisely the presence of concepts in perceptions. For some schools and authors, any perception is by definition indeterminate, stemming from the contact between an object (be it external or mental) and the senses.

Other thinkers held the opposite view: perception is certainly sense-based but it always involves, in all cases, a conceptualisation.

Finally, there is a third, intermediate view, which conceives perception as a two-stage process, where a first immediate moment is followed by a subsequent conceptualisation. According to what one can call the "standard picture", the immediate nature of perception is defended, albeit in very different ways, by the old Nyāya and the Buddhists. The determinate nature of all knowledge is on the other hand championed by Bhartṛhari, the Jainas, the Pratyabhijñā and the Navya-Nyāya.

Finally, the intermediate position is adopted by the Mīmāṃsā, some Nyāya authors, and the Advaita Vedānta.

The purpose of this panel is to reassess the problem of conceptuality in perception by considering different case studies. In general, the panel will examine the following questions.

1) Is the "standard picture" always applicable? Or are there cases that defy what one would normally expect?
2) Is it possible to establish historical relations between the views different authors had on the problem at stake? In other words, is it possible to reconstruct a history of the notion of conceptuality in perception in the philosophy of premodern South Asia?
3) When different interpretations emerge within the same school, what are the reasons to justify the shift from a position to another (sometimes the opposite one)?
4) What is the value of the arguments that thinkers of different persuasions put forward? Is there any "best" philosophical definition of perception?

All contributions seek therefore to marry a philological approach with a philosophical one. Starting from textual material, the participants will evaluate both the historical implications of their case studies and the philosophical value of the arguments they discuss.

Jack Beaulieu
Raghunātha on seeing darkness

ABSTRACT

Nyāya philosophers maintain that we literally see absence (*abhāva*). Most early Nyāya philosophers additionally maintain that we only epistemically (*savikalpaka*) see absence: we always see that the counterpositive (*pratiyogin*) is absent.

As Gaṅgeśa (c. 1320) claims, we are always aware of the absence along with its counterpositive (*sapratiyogika*). We never see absence without any awareness of what is absent, but rather always see that the pot is not there or that the cloth is not there. Gaṅgeśa, who never saw a piano, never saw the absence of the piano in his room.

Raghunātha (c. 1510) eschews this tradition to argue that we can non-epistemically (*nirvikalpaka*) see absence: we sometimes see absence without any awareness of what is absent. He appeals to perception of darkness (*tamas*). Darkness is the result of many absent light sources, but agents see darkness without any awareness of the light sources that are blocked.

Amit Chaturvedi
Tracing the evolution of Buddhist and Nyāya views on non-conceptual perception

ABSTRACT

This paper seeks to explain one of the few points on which Buddhist and Nyāya philosophers actually came to an agreement — namely, that non-conceptual perceptions (*nirvikalpakapratyakṣa*) are states of awareness which do not involve any attribution of names or predicative properties to objects (*nāmajātyādiyojanārahita*).

I trace the evolution of Buddhist and Nyāya views on *nirvikalpaka-pratyakṣa*, and claim that there is a common trend in their development from Vasubandhu to Dignāga, and from Vātsyāyana to Vācaspati Miśra and Gaṅgeśa. That trend, I suggest, can be illuminated with a distinction made in contemporary discussions of non-conceptual content between "state non-conceptualism" and "content non-conceptualism". On my reading, both Buddhist and Nyāya thinkers ultimately shifted from presuming state non-conceptualism to advocating forms of content non-conceptualism. To explain this shift, I cite two philosophical and exegetical reasons.

First, contemporary defenders of non-conceptualism have argued that the state view is ultimately untenable, and collapses into a content view. Second, Buddhists and Naiyāyikas came to view concept-possession as grounded upon the operation of memory-traces (*saṃskāra*), rather than on linguistic mastery. With this refined theory of concept-possession, the line between non-conceptual and concept-laden states was preservable only through positing an essential difference between non-conceptual and conceptual contents.

Finally, I examine how, even having reached a shared definition of *nirvikalpaka* perception, the different theoretical commitments of Navya Nyāya and Buddhism led to a divergence over the conscious character of non-conceptual states. This divergence motivates us to consider how the conceptual structure of perceptual contents may be linked with their availability to consciousness.

Pei-Lin Chiou
Kamalaśīla's epistemological-soteriological understanding of the non-conceptuality of yogic perception

ABSTRACT

The eighth-century Buddhist philosopher Kamalaśīla (ca. 740–795) was not only a learned epistemologist but also versed in Buddhist soteriology. In his treatises on Buddhist spiritual practice, such as the Bhāvanākramas, he presents a theory of the Buddhist path that incorporates the epistemological idea of yogic perception (*yogipratyakṣa*), which had been developed in the Buddhist *pramāṇa* tradition. According to this theory, yogic perception is equivalent to the soteriological concept of non-conceptual gnosis (*nirvikalpajñāna*). This theory thus provides us the possibility to answer questions regarding yogic perception from a soteriological angle.

In the present paper, I shall explore Kamalaśīla's understanding of the non-conceptuality of yogic perception by examining his account of non-conceptual gnosis. I will demonstrate how Kamalaśīla's view of such perception could meet the epistemological definition of perception as free of conceptual construction.

Patrick McAllister
Acting without knowledge?
Prajñākaragupta's alternative to Dharmottara

ABSTRACT

From the beginning, Buddhist epistemologists defined perception as non-conceptual. Dharmakīrti's redevelopment of Dignāga's philosophical system made it apparent that there is a problem in this approach: perception was said to be a means of valid cognition, and a means of valid cognition was defined as imparting a cognition that allows a person to act successfully. Yet how could perception fulfil this role if it is not conceptual? Surely, any action presupposes a conscious judgement. But how could there be a non-conceptual judgement?

It seems that this tension, largely unanswered in Dharmakīrti's writings, did not go unnoticed by his two most ambitious commentators, Dharmottara and Prajñākaragupta. Where the former essentially admits to a "conceptual perception", the latter provided a systematic answer that seeks to avoid this conclusion. Their widely divergent solutions to this problem will be presented in this paper.

Shishir Saxena
The Prābhākara's claim of the middle-path: Śālikanātha on *nirvikalpaka* cognitions

ABSTRACT

The ninth century Mīmāṃsā philosopher Śālikanātha is often considered to be the most important of Prābhākara thinkers, and in his *Prakaraṇapañcikā*, a text comprising fourteen essays (verses and commentary), two essays — *Amṛtakalā* (AK) and *Pramāṇapārāyaṇa* (PP) — discuss the Prābhākara doctrine of perception. Śālikanātha defines perception as *sākṣāt pratītiḥ* 'a direct apprehension' (AK v.4) and his analysis of this, often referred to as the *tripuṭīpratyakṣavāda*, distinguishes between its three constituents: the perceived object (*meya*), the perceiving subject (*mātṛ*) and the perceptual cognition (*pramā*).

Śālikanātha, while discussing this third constituent in his PP, evaluates the topic of non-conceptual (*nirvikalpaka*) and conceptual (*savikalpaka*) cognitions and presents several arguments to distinguish and defend his doctrine against those of not only the Naiyāyikas and Buddhists but in fact the Bhāṭṭa Mīmāṃsakas as well.

In this paper, I consider some of these arguments and demonstrate Śālikanātha's defence and unique understanding of *nirvikalpaka* cognitions, and thereby consider the case whether his doctrine can be rightly labelled a "golden mean" (Jha 1942: 95) between the Buddhists and the Bhāṭṭa Mīmāṃsakas.

REFERENCES

Jha, G. 1942. *Pūrva Mīmāmsā in Its Sources*. Benares: Benares Hindu University.

The language of things:
Materiality as a fruitful lens in the Humanities

Conveners: Borayin Larios and Nina Mirnig

In this panel, we will explore some of the advantages and limitations of considering materiality as an important focal point in a number of disciplines in the humanities. The theoretical and methodological approach often referred to as the "material turn" gives us the opportunity to work from a perspective that is still often neglected in disciplines such as philology, philosophy as well as religious and cultural history in South Asian studies. What if we considered materiality not as secondary to ideas, but as an actant that triggers ideas, states of mind, and specific practices? What happens if, for example, we work with the assumption that objects, their usage, valuation, and power of attraction are inseparable from culture and from practices embedded in these cultures?

When we, for instance, consider texts as integral part of the objects that transmit them and treat them as artifacts that can "do things" and thereby go beyond a purely text-based analysis divorced from the material context?

How can this approach contribute to our understanding about texts, ideas, and practices?

How can disciplines such as archaeology, philology or anthropology effectively enter into such "arranged marriages" by using materiality as a common ground without diluting the boundaries of each discipline?

Borayin Larios
Textuality, performativity, and materiality: the case of Gaṇeśa from the brahmin's mouth to the streets.

ABSTRACT

In this presentation, I will be exploring the Hindu God Gaṇeśa to illustrate how an interdisciplinary approach can be fruitful.

First, I will use the text called *Gaṇapatyatharvaśirṣopaniṣat* as an example of Gaṇeśa's textuality. This *Upaniṣad* lends itself to illuminating a broad phenomenon in Sanskrit literature: the relationship between innovation and maintenance of earlier forms and content of knowledge and aesthetic expression to create new works.

Second, I will address the performative aspect of this text to discuss socioreligious change within Hinduism. Thus, the ritual application and performance of this text in contemporary Maharashtra especially in the context of the annual Gaṇeśa festival.

As a final conceptual lens, I will consider Gaṇeśas materiality and spatial production in the context of urban religion as it finds expression today in the city of Pune. This will hopefully illustrate how a combined methodological approach can enrich the study of contemporary Hinduism.

Christèle Barois
On some philological questions arising from the observation of Śaiva rituals

ABSTRACT

During a long stay in South India (2003–2007), I had the opportunity to observe temple rituals and ceremonies (Tamil Nadu, Andhra Pradesh, Karnataka). At that same period, I was translating the sections on the daily, occasional and optional rites of the *Vāyavīyasaṃhitā* (11th c.), a South-Indian Śaiva text, and I was participating in the critical edition of the *Dīptāgama*, a late medieval treatise on installations (*pratiṣṭhātantra*).

The confrontation of my on-going philological work with the observation of the contemporary implementation of Śaivāgamas and medieval ritual manuals (*paddhadi*) provided me with a point of support to understand ritual texts, as well as it generated new questions both on the nature and form of these texts and on their application.

In this lecture, I will give a few examples of questions, from texts to materiality and vice versa, arising from the observation of specific Śaiva rituals, in particular the initiation and consecration of a Śaiva master (2005), performed according to the procedure taught in the *Kriyākramadyotikā*, a *Śaivasiddhānta* manual dating from the 12th century.

Verena Widorn
Materiality and visibility of textual sources
at a pilgrimage center in Himachal Pradesh, India

ABSTRACT

The historical reality of a community's ritual traditions and worship practices does not necessarily coincide with the meaning of the written and material evidence as analyzed, interpreted, and postulated by scholars. Texts may be lost, inscriptions may fade, building structures may be altered, and original forms may be rendered unrecognizable. The knowledge of such changes is rarely retrievable by the believers, besides being to a large extent less relevant to them. Although the legitimation of a site, building, or sculpture as an object of worship is primarily established through material or textual evidence, which at best reveals a religious-historical development over centuries for the researcher, the development of local rites of veneration usually takes place on a different level.

As a case study, this paper presents three different textual documents closely connected to the temple complex of Triloknath, a small, but important pilgrimage center in the remote Chandrabhaga Valley in Lahul, Himachal Pradesh. The place is a sacred site for both, Hindus and Buddhists, and visited particularly on the occasion of an annual festival and fair, but also in order to pray for fertility.

The paper discusses the meaning of the three texts — a Śāradā inscription dated to the 9th century CE, a travelogue from a Buddhist pilgrim of the 17th century CE, and a Tibetan *māhātmya* from 1905 — in terms of their reference to Avalokiteśvara and his materialization as the main devotional image of the shrine.

While the texts are little known, the white marble sculpture of uncertain date has become a famous supra-regional object of worship and is even venerated by Hindus as Śiva, Lord of the Three Worlds (*Trilokanath*).

Nina Mirnig
Of cakras, deer and tridents: Sanskrit inscriptions as material culture in Early Medieval Nepal

ABSTRACT

The reign of the Licchavi kings in the Kathmandu Valley from ca. the 3rd to at least the 8th century CE is often characterized as an economic and cultural heyday. An important element associated with the region's cultural development at this time is the introduction of Sanskrit literacy, the earliest extant material evidence of which is a single one-line inscription of the 2nd or 3rd century CE, followed by a collection of over 200 inscriptions issued between the 5th to the mid-8th century, the so-called corpus of Licchavi inscriptions.

While the rich textual content of the inscriptions has received and continues to attract much scholarly attention, analyses of their material aspects have thus far been neglected.

In this paper, I will look at these inscriptions through the lens of materiality and focus, in particular, on the epigraphic practices related to the most common type of Licchavi-period epigraphy: the free-standing stone slab inscription. By complementing the textual analysis with an investigation of the inscriptions' materiality as reflected by scribal practices, material context and non-verbal elements that communicate beyond the written word — such as the characteristic symbols of cakras, deer and tridents — I will aim to develop a more comprehensive reconstruction of the inscriptions' function and usage, as well as the degrees of literacy of the intended audiences.

Raphaël Voix
Bharata's immortals: inclusivism and egalitarian pluralism in sectarian Hinduism

ABSTRACT

For the last twenty years or so, it has not been uncommon to encounter in India a type of image that seems to borrow from the theological inclusivism of caste-based Hinduism while referring to sectarian divine figures. This type of image features male saints of different sectarian affiliations side by side, albeit all from religious communities that originated in South Asia. It gives the impression of a "class photo" of ascetics. These images are more prevalent in northern India, and probably originated in Bengal; they are found particularly in places of worship dedicated to a saint. However, they are not the object of a cult and no type of ritual seems to be associated with them.

How are they produced? What is their function? What does this type of image tell us about the relationship between materiality and ideology in contemporary Hinduism?

By establishing a social biography (Appadurai 1986) of one of these images, this paper will attempt to understand the logics at stake behind its genesis and its ongoing variations and thus contribute to understanding its material production.

REFERENCES

Appadurai, A. (ed.). 1986. *The Social Life of Things. Commodities in Cultural Perspective.* Cambridge: Cambridge University Press.

Telling tales, interpreting documents:
the interaction of literary and historical practices

Conveners: Naresh Keerthi and Elena Mucciarelli

Panel's overview

In a talk given in honour of Israel Yuval, great scholar of Jewish History, Avraham B. Yehoshua complained that historians have lost their capacity to look for the big picture: they are satisfied with petty studies into tiny, allegedly insignificant subjects. He then gave the example of Theodor Herzel: a writer who made history [sic]. Is then Literature or Literary Studies the path to write History in a meaningful way? Philologists likewise have been accused of focusing on too narrow issues. Moreover, they seem to neglect the people behind the texts and their relation to larger orders of culture, society, and polity. Their reading of the sources is missing a sense of historicity. Some of these accusations might well result from partial representations of the research fields and deranged visions of academy.

Nevertheless, there are some questions worth asking in relation to the discursive practices of historians and philologists both relying on narrative. This panel will try to address some of them.

- How do we negotiate the narrative and discursive devices of our material? How do we evaluate and read a text?
- As part of a historical process or as literary composition bereft of any connection to the life of the author?
- How do we historicise anonymous texts? Or those whose authors are mere names, with no details of the author's provenance being forthcoming?
- When trying to make sense of a text are we to ask questions about the individual and his sensibility or about the social groups that created the environment for that text?
- What kind of hermeneutic would we get if historian and philologist (textual studies scholar) were to respectively read pieces of literature and historical accounts with their different perspectives?
- Texts can be classified both as historical documents and as products of a specific aesthetic: can the two classifications come together in a broader paradigm?

Talia Ariav
The trope and the world: patterns of individuality in Sanskrit literature from the Kaveri Delta, 17–18th centuries

ABSTRACT

Sanskrit authors generally refrain from writing themselves into their works. They rarely speak in the first person, and when they do, it is often done through sedimented tropes and genre-bound patterns.

In this talk, I will reflect on instances of encoded autobiographical remarks in works of the early modern poet Nīlakaṇṭha Dīkṣita, his student Rāmabhadra Dīkṣita, and their affiliated students and colleagues from around Thanjavur.

I will be sampling these authors' distinct versions of the tropes of the first per- son, found in their prologues and hymns to gods.

I suggest that these tropes were ideal spaces for these authors to fashion themselves in, as they provided them with the language to index their lives through an intended game of shadows. Listening to these moments carefully and inter-textually reveals much about the lives of these authors, including their intellectual, religious and familial commitments, the economical structures that sustained their work, and what mattered to them.

Further, these instances allow us to glimpse these authors' discreet notions of individuality and selfhood. These moments build on the productive tension between the conventional and the unique, which lies at the heart of these au- thors' notions and practices of authorship. They pose a self that is not divorced from convention, but is rather composed of it, intimately bound with the tradi- tions in which one writes and lives.

Sivan Goren-Arzony
God's slaves, dancers or prostitutes?
Toward a nuanced reading of Early Maṇipravāḷam heroines

ABSTRACT

Matriliny was a common practice in various communities across the Indian ocean. It was convenient, according to Kerala historian Mahmood Kooria, in oceanic households, where travel was a common way of life. In Kerala, up until the 1920s, matriliny was normative among more than twenty different communities. Yet, most of those, including the large Nair community, shared very little connection to maritime trade or to life on the sea.

Matriarchal houses were the basic reference point of Kerala's early Maṇipravāḷam literature. While other South Asian vernaculars often commence with adaptations of Sanskrit texts, early Maṇipravāḷam depicts and praises local heroines, represented in their own worlds: their imagined genealogies, the splendor of their bodies and houses, and the lively presence of their many admirers. These women have many labels in scholarship: *devadāsīs*, courtesans, dancers, and prostitutes, among others.

Devadāsīs are a common trope in Sanskrit literature all around South Asia; Early Maṇipravāḷam literature itself seems to be referencing to some of these representations.

And yet, is describing a courtesan in a literary text that depicts a matrilineal world the same as it is in a patrilineal world? Can we read these heroines in a nuanced way, combining what we know of Kerala's history and Sanskrit literature? Is *devadāsī* even the right term?

In my talk, I will address these questions, among others, by presenting descriptions of several early Maṇipravāḷam heroines.

Naresh Keerthi
Bending and blending tales: Ranna's alchemy of Kannada poetical genres

ABSTRACT

A tenth century jaina poet Ranna (ca. 1000 CE) wrote a poem in Old Kannada, in a strange genre that declares that it will "equate" the poet's patron — the Caḷukya prince Sattiga to the epic hero Bhīma, and tell his tale. While Ranna did not invent this genre, his Victorious Bhima (*Sāhasa-bhīma-vijayaṃ*) is probably the most popular example of a classical Kannada text that presents a pastiche with patches of historical and biographical details of Sattiga surfacing in a text that otherwise retells the well-known tale from the Mahabharata. This text and others like it present unusual notions of praise, narrative structure and identity — imbricated in the cusp of poetics and politics.

Abhilash Malayil
Mī(n)māṃsa: fish-meat, Naṃbūtiri ritual and the early modern political conflict in *Cāttirāṅkaṃ*

ABSTRACT

Cāttirāṅkam (also known as *Sanghakaḷi*) is one of the obscured artforms of the Malayalam-speaking Brahmins or the Nambūdiri. It was often referred to as a "new" variety of ritual performance involving group-dance, formalized acting and utterance, and is staged exclusively by ordained groups (*yōgam*) of young Nambūdiri men. The site of performance has also marinated a visible trait of exclusivity that *Cāttirāṅkam* was always staged in (aristocratic) Brahmin households (of southern Malabar and of the Princely Cochin) on certain ceremonial occasions and viewed exclusively by a group of the commensal Nambūdiri audience. *Cāttirāṅkam* performers combine aesthetic and textual elements that have been adapted, and at times found improvised, from a diverse set of (early)-Medieval sources. They include the antique routines of the *Vēda* chanting prevalent in Kerala, foundational stories remembered in Purāṇic and *Kēraḷōlpatti* corpuses, the custom of music and dance patronized in Keralite temples, theatrical aspects of the regional drama (*nāṭakam*) and martial arts, and certain highly stylized verbal formulae of the royal Grandhavari prose as well as the localized folk-satire.

This paper will examine the literary texts of *Cāttirāṅkam* or the *Cātṛāṅkasārārṇavam* and argue that a significant section of them were either composed during or had been informed by an important early modern political conflict.

Vyākaraṇa and its many espouses: Linguistics, Philology, Philosophy

Convener: Artemij Keidan

Panel's overview

The main assumption of the present panel is that *vyākaraṇa* and many of the contemporary disciplines dealing with language, such as linguistics strictly speaking, but also philology, textual criticism, philosophy of language, are tightly bound by reciprocal connections, some of which go back even to the very beginning of the western "discovery" of Sanskrit together with its traditional grammatical description. Accordingly, a comparative approach to *vyākaraṇa* and the modern language sciences is revealing in two ways.

From the one hand, *vyākaraṇa* teaches us something on Sanskrit (historically, it taught us almost everything about it), and, more generally, on the theoretical linguistics and philosophy of language.

But, on the other hand, contemporary linguistics itself often becomes useful in analyzing *vyakarana*. Not only it helps understanding the essence of the traditional Sanskrit grammars, but it also provides some tools for investigating its historical development and transformation, as well as for deciphering the mysteries of its written tradition.

The present panel has, therefore, the purpose of challenging the two sides of this bilateral — or rather, one-to-many — relationship favoring a compenetrative analysis of both.

Anuja Ajotikar
Issues in nominal derivation in Pāṇini, *Kātantra* and *Cāndra* grammar: the case of *idam* and *adas* pronouns

ABSTRACT

Declensions and conjugations form a major part of grammar. This derivational part of the grammar is a systematic and, at the same time, abstract system. Root words and list of suffixes are the basic input material for the derivation. As a common user of a language, this knowledge, i.e. division of a word into base word and suffix, is unknown, but at the same time, the user cognizes certain forms with certain roots. They relate various forms present in the language with each other. Unquestionably, it is just an understanding of usage and relations between various forms of a word and the difference in meaning. For example in English 'I' means the first person, but forms like me, myself and mine are also related to the first person. They are used in different context and also depending on the sentence structure. The analysis of the usage and also the forms is a subject of grammar.

Regarding Sanskrit, as an ancient language, the scientific systematization in linguistic studies began with the grammar of Pāṇini. Works like *Pratiśākhya* and *Nirukta* have pursued some analysis of the Sanskrit Language, but they are not as comprehensive as the grammar of Pāṇini. This is the oldest available complete and comprehensive grammar in the history of Sanskrit. Sanskrit grammars which were composed after Pāṇini are also reached to us more or less intact. There are eleven grammars of Sanskrit including the Pāṇinian grammar.

Sanskrit is highly inflectional language. It is morphologically rich in nature. Pāṇini's description of Sanskrit morphology is unique and has been studied for many years. Pāṇini while describing the morphology it is observed that he arrives at a step where any further distinction of a word form is stoped and the stage is taken as a basis for the rule based derivational process. There are two main basic units in the derivation namely *dhātu* and *prātipadika*. It has been observed that these basic roots or forms are accepted without question in post-Pāṇinian grammatical systems also. But the question arises: why is the particular choice made to begin the derivation process by a Sanskrit grammarian and why not any other?

This query started with the rules describing derivation of first person and second person pronouns in the Pāṇinian grammar. Pāṇini has spent a lot material for the derivation of the first person and second person pronouns. As a case study, these two pronouns indeed form a unique example, but in general the derivation of pronouns is complicated, especially those pronouns which end in consonants, such as *idam*, and *adas*. This paper is an extension of my doctoral thesis *Issues in Nominal declension in Traditional Sanskrit grammars with special reference to 1st person and 2nd person pronouns*. The thesis aimed at investigating the root selection principle. The study concluded that while selecting the root-word, preference is given to the longer unit as reduction in the root-word is thought to be simpler than addition. The accent of the root word has also importance in the derivation process. The current effort is to check how those findings are applicable to other root-word and suffix choices made by, or accepted by, Pāṇini. The comparative study assisted in determining whether any non-Pāṇinian and post-Pāṇinian grammarians made notable changes and also attempted to begin the derivation by selecting different bases for the derivation process.

This paper will go over the general characteristics of *idam* and *adas* pronouns as well as the rules for deriving the 21 declensional forms. This paper will also compare derivation process given in Pāṇinian grammar with the derivation process given in the *Kātantra* and *Cāndra* grammar.

REFERENCES

Abhyankar, K. V. (ed.). 1951. *Vyākaraṇamahābhāṣya of Patañjali*. Vol. 6. Marathi translation. Pune: Deccan Education Society.

Abhyankar, K. V. (ed.). 1954. *Vyākaraṇamahābhāṣya of Patañjali*, vol 7, *Prastāvanā Khanda*. Pune: Deccan Education Society.

Abhyankar, K. V. (ed.). 1967. *Paribhāṣāsangraha (a collection of original works on Vyākaraṇa Paribhāṣās)*. Poona: Bhandarkar Orintal Research Institute.

Abhyankar, K. V. (ed.). 2001. *Svaraprakriyā by Rāmacandra with Svopajñavyākhyā*. Pune: Anandashram Samstha.

Abhyankar, K. V., and J. M. Shukla. 1986. *A dictionary of Sanskrit Grammar*. Baroda: The Oriental Institute.

Ajotikar, A. P. 2013. *Issues in Nominal declension in Traditional Sanskrit grammars with special reference to 1st person and 2nd person pronouns*. Indian Institute of Technology, Bombay, Powai India (Unpublished Doctoral thesis).

Belvelkar, S. K. 1997. *Systems of Sanskrit Grammar*. Delhi: The Bharatiya Book Corporation.

Bhate, S. 1978. "Non Paninian Systems of Sanskrit Grammar vis-a-vis Pāṇini: External vowel sandhi". *Centre of Advanced Study in Sanskrit* 4: 80–96.

Caturveda, Giridharasharma & Parameshvaranandasharma (ed.). 1995. *Vaiyā-karaṇasiddhāntakaumudī with Bālamanoramā and Tattvabodhinī*. Delhi: Motilal Banarasidass.

Chatterji, K. C. (ed.). 1953. *Cāndra Vyākarana*. Part I. Poona: Deccan College Post graduate and Research Institute.

Chatterji, K. C. (ed.). 1961. *Cāndra Vyākarana*. Part II. Poona: Deccan College Post graduate and Research Institute.

Śāstrī, D. (ed.). 2010. *Kātantrarūpamālā*. Śrīmahāvīrajī: Jainavidyā Saṃsthāna.

Liebich, B. (ed.). 1918. *Candra-Vṛtti. Der Original-Kommentar Candragomin's zu seinem grammatischen Sūtra*. Leibzig: Abhandlungen für dieKunde des Morgenlandes.

Saini, R. S. (ed.). 1987. *Kātantra vyākarana*. Delhi: Bharatiya Vidya Prakashan.

Tanuja Ajotikar
Analysis of counter examples on *Aṣṭādhyāyī* 1.4.33–38

ABSTRACT

Counter examples are an important part of commentaries on rules in the *Aṣṭādhyāyī*. Ajotikar et. al. (2016) conclude that the essential feature of a counter example is that it have all the conditions stated in the rule except one (*ekāṅgavikalatā*). Ajotikar (2021: forthcoming) discusses how a variant reading for a counter example helps to understand the relation between two operational rules. This article added one more aspect to the importance of counter examples. However, there are some cases where the purpose of the counter example is not clear. In the present paper I study counter examples provided on the *sūtras* A 1.4.33–38, in the *kāraka* section, on which Patañjali did not comment. These *sūtras* are chosen for the discussion because the counter examples available on these *sūtras* are first provided only in the *Kāśikāvṛtti*.

The paper is divided in several sections. First section of the paper surveys almost all of the commentaries on the *Aṣṭādhyāyī*. Then the data available from non-Pāṇinian grammars on similar *sūtras* are discussed. Second section discusses what do the counter examples on these rules imply. The third section discusses what Bhartṛhari says on these rules. It is examined whether these counter examples comply with Bhartṛhari's discussion. In the fourth section it is discussed how modern translations deal with these counter examples. A few samples of translation are analyzed. The last section is the conclusion of the paper.

Let us discuss one example. A 1.4.33 रुच्यर्थानां प्रीयमाणः "The technical term *sampradāna* denotes one who is pleased (*prīyamāṇaḥ*) in relation to the verbal stem having the sense of 'to please' (*ruci=arthānām*)". The counter example for the condition *prīyamāṇa* is provided following *prīyamāṇaḥ kim* "Why the term *prīyamāṇa* 'the person pleased' is added in the rule?"

1)   *devadattāya rocate modakaḥ pathi*
     "Devadatta likes sweet-meats on the way".

When we apply the feature of the counter example (Ajotikar et. al. 2016), it implies that in the absence of the term *prīyamāṇa*, as the only one recurring term available in this rule is *kāraka*, the rule would mean any *kāraka* in relation to the verb *ruc* 'to please' would become *sampradāna* and *pathin* 'path' would get the term *sampradāna* and if *anabhihita* would get dative case. Thus in the sentence, *devadattāya rocate modakaḥ pathi*, the word *pathi* would not be in locative case.

The term *kāraka* comes under the scope of the heading A 1.4.1 आ कडारादेका संज्ञा and A 1.4.2 विप्रतिषेधे परं कार्यम् 1.4.2. The *kāraka* term stated by a later rule overrides the previous rule. Thus any *kāraka* stated after the *sampradāna* would override the *sampradāna* in the absence of any other special condition. It is not proper to explain that, in the absence of the condition *prīyamāṇa*, *pathi* would not be termed *adhikaraṇa* and would be in locative case. On the contrary the word *pathin* 'path' should be termed *adhikaraṇa* and should be in locative case because the term *adhikaraṇa* is stated by A 1.4.45 which is a later rule. It is suffice to say that the counter example involving the *adhikaraṇa* here falls short to explain the real purpose of the condition *prīyamāṇa*. Since Patañjali did not comment on rules A 1.4.33–41, the source for the counter example is the *Kāśikāvṛtti*. It is interesting to examine how later commentators provide counter example on these rules. Table 1 (next page) provides such data.

The table 1 shows that the counter examples as given in the *Kāśikāvṛtti* are repeated by others. There is only one special case, A 1.4.34 where a variant reading is found in *Kāśikāvṛtti*'s Osmania edition (p. 82, fn 10) *devadattaḥ ślāghate* 'Devadatta praises', *devadattaṁ ślāghate* 's/he praises Devadatta". These two variant readings are provided by Haradatta in the *Padamañjarī*. Haradatta quotes *devadattaḥ ślāghate* as the main reading and notes variant *devadattaṁ ślāghate*. He does not attest the counter example accepted in the main text of the Osmania edition. These two counter examples are not mentioned in any other commentary. I will discuss these counter examples and their significance in detail in the paper.

Bhartr̥hari in the *Vākyapadīya* (*Sādhanasamuddeśa* verse 130) discusses these rules. In the table 2 (next page), I give the list of rules of which A 1.4.33–41 are exception to according to Bhartr̥hari. In the absence of these rules what could be the alternate form possible is explained by Bhartr̥hari.

We do not find any counter example on the above rules that take into consideration Bhartr̥hari's discussion.

NON-PĀṆINIAN GRAMMARS
Most of the cases of *sampradāna* are covered by *tādarthya*. When desired as direct object, as in *devadattaṁ ślāghate* 's/he praises Devadatta' or *puṣpāṇi spr̥hayati* 's/he desires flowers', are valid expressions as per the *Cān-*

					Table 1
Aṣṭādhyāyī	Kāśikāvṛtti	Bhāṣā-vṛtti	Rūpāvatāra	Prakriyā Kaumudī	Siddhānta Kaumudī
A 1.4.33 रुच्यर्थानां प्रीयमाणः	प्रीयमाण इति किम्. देवदत्ताय रोचते मोदकः पथि.	—	प्रीयमाण इति किम्. देवदत्ताय रोचते मोदकः पथि.	—	प्रीयमाण इति किम्. देवदत्ताय रोचते मोदकः पथि.
A 1.4.34 श्लाघह्नुङ्स्थाशपां ज्ञीप्स्यमानः	ज्ञीप्स्यमान इति किम्. देवदत्ताय श्लाघते पथि	—	—	—	ज्ञीप्स्यमान इति किम्. देवदत्ताय श्लाघते पथि
A 1.4.35 धारेरुत्तमर्णः	उत्तमर्ण इति किम्. देवदत्ताय शतं धारयति ग्रामे.	—	—	—	उत्तमर्ण इति किम्. देवदत्ताय शतं धारयति ग्रामे.
A 1.4.36 स्पृहेरीप्सितः	ईप्सित इति किम्. पुष्पेभ्यो वने स्पृहयति.	—	ईप्सित इति किम्. पुष्पेभ्यो स्पृहयति वने.	—	ईप्सित इति किम्. पुष्पेभ्यो वने स्पृहयति.
A 1.4.37 क्रुधद्रुहेर्ष्यासूयार्थानां यं प्रति कोपः	यं प्रति कोप इति किं भार्यामीर्ष्यति	—	यं प्रति कोप इति किं भार्यामीर्ष्यति	यं प्रति कोप इति किं भार्यामीर्ष्यति	यं प्रति कोप इति किं भार्यामीर्ष्यति
A 1.4.38 क्रुधद्रुहोरुपसृष्ट्योः कर्म	उपसृष्ट्योरिति किम्. देवदत्ताय क्रुध्यति, यज्ञदत्ताय द्रुह्यति.	—	—	—	—
A 1.4.39 राधीक्ष्योर्यस्य विप्रश्नः	—	—	—	—	—
A 1.4.40 प्रत्याङ्भ्यां श्रुवः पूर्वस्य कर्ता	—	—	—	—	—
A 1.4.41 अनुप्रतिगृणश्च	—	—	—	—	—

	Table 2
sūtra no.	Exception to
A 1.4.33 रुच्यर्थानां प्रीयमाणः	A 1.4.55 तत्प्रयोजको हेतुश्च
A 1.4.34 श्लाघह्नुङ्स्थाशपां ज्ञीप्स्यमानः	A 1.4.49 कर्तुरीप्सिततमं कर्म
A 1.4.35 धारेरुत्तमर्णः	A 2.3.50 षष्ठी शेषे
A 1.4.36 स्पृहेरीप्सितः	A 1.4.49 कर्तुरीप्सिततमं कर्म
A 1.4.37 क्रुधद्रुहेर्ष्यासूयार्थानां यं प्रति कोपः	A 1.4.49 कर्तुरीप्सिततमं कर्म
A 1.4.38 क्रुधद्रुहोरुपसृष्ट्योः कर्म	Not discussed
A 1.4.39 राधीक्ष्योर्यस्य विप्रश्नः	A 1.4.55 तत्प्रयोजको हेतुश्च
A 1.4.40 प्रत्याङ्भ्यां श्रुवः पूर्वस्य कर्ता	A 1.4.55 तत्प्रयोजको हेतुश्च
A 1.4.41 अनुप्रतिगृणश्च	A 1.4.55 तत्प्रयोजको हेतुश्च

dravṛtti. No counter example is provided in the *Cāndravṛtti* on rules which state the *sampradāna* term. *Jainendra vyākaraṇa* provides a counter examples as *devadattāya śataṁ dhārayati daridraḥ* 'A poor man holds 100 for Devadatta'. *śākaṭāyana vyākaraṇa* made *spṛherīpsitaḥ* optional so that *puṣpāṇi spṛhayati* 's/he desires flowers' is also considered a valid expression. There is no counter example provided which matches with any counter example in the *Kāśikāvṛtti*.

Translations in English, Hindi and Marathi provide some explanation to the counter examples on these rules, but fail to describe their significance.

1.   S. C. Vasu: «why do we say the person pleased? Observe 'देवदत्ताय...'. Devadatta likes sweet-meat in the way. The word 'पथिन्' is here in the 7th case» (p. 348).

2.   Sharadaranjan Ray: «why 'प्रीयमाण'? Witness 'देवदत्ताय...' etc. where 'पथिन्' way feels no pleasure and takes आधारे सप्तमी» (p. 59).

3.   श्रीधरानंद घिल्डियाल: «'प्रीयमाण' (पसन्द करने वाला) पद का ग्रहण यहां क्यों किया गया? इस प्रश्न के द्वारा प्रीयमाण पद के प्रयोजन (कृत्य) को प्रकट करने का आधार उपस्थित करते है । 'देवदत्ताय रोचते मोदकः पथि ।' (देवदत्त को मार्ग मे लड्डु अच्छे लगते है, पसंद आते है।) इस वाक्य मे 'पथि' की sampradāna संज्ञा नही हुई । क्यों की पसंद करनेवाला मार्ग नही, वह तो आधार है। अतः adhikaraṇa सप्तमी विभक्ति उससे आती है। यहां प्रीयमाण देवदत्त है, उसकी sampradāna संज्ञा होती है।» (p. 94).

4.   जयशंकरलाल त्रिपाठी-सुधाकर मालवीयः «'प्रीयमाणः (प्रीति का आश्रय = प्रसन्न होने वाला)' यह किस लिये है? देवदत्ताय रोचते मोदकः पथि । (देवदत्त को रास्ते में लड्डु अच्छा लगता है ।) (यहां पन्था प्रीयमाण नही है अतः उसकी sampradāna संज्ञा नही होती ।)» (p. 146).

5.   म. दा. साठेः «सूत्रात 'प्रीयमाण' असे पद का घातले? 'देवदत्ताय रोचते मोदकः पथि' या वाक्यात 'देवदत्त' 'प्रीयमाण' आहे 'पथिन्' नाही». (p. 94).

CONCLUSION

The feature discussed of a counter example (Ajotikar et. al. 2016) is true to most of the cases but where it comes the issue of complex semantic conditions, it is difficult to justify the usefulness of the available counter examples on A 1.4.33–38. These must be included as a procedure of completing criteria for a commentary but they fail to describe the significance of semantic conditions for which they are provided.

REFERENCES

Ajotikar, T. 2021. "रुरुदिव–रुरुदिम or रुदिवः–रुदिमः Which is a proper set of counter example on A 7.2.8?" उशती (UGC care listed) 2020, Rashtriya Sanskrit Sansthan, Ganganath Jha Campus, Prayagaraj. (Forthcoming).

Ajotikar, T., M. Kulkarni, and P. M. Scharf. 2016. "Counterexamples (*pratyudāharaṇa*) in Pāṇinian grammar", in G. Cardona, H. Ogawa (eds.), *Vyākaraṇaparipṛcchā: Proceedings of the Vyākaraṇa section of the 16th World Sanskrit Conference*, pp. 23–52. New Delhi: D. K. Publishers.

Ray, K., and Sh. Ray (eds.). 1965. वैयाकरणसिद्धान्तकौमुदी. Calcutta: K. C. Neogi & Nababihakar Press.

Sarma, V. S., and Ś. Pullela (eds.). 1985–1986. *Nyāsaparākhyā Kāśikāvivaraṇapañjikā*. Hyderabad: Sanskrit Academy, Osmania University.

Sathe, M. D. Vol. I, (संज्ञा–परिभाषा kāraka आणि समास), मराठी भाषांतर, पुणे: संस्कृत विद्या परिसंस्था.

Sharma, A., Kh. Deshpande, and D. G. Padhye (eds.). 1969–1970. *Kāśikā: A Commentary on Pāṇini's Grammar*. Hyderabad: Osmania University.

Śrīrāmacanduḍu, P., and V. Sundaraśarman (eds.). 1981. *The Padamañjarı by Haradatta Miśra: a commentary on the Kāśikā of Vāmana and Jayāditya*. Hyderabad: Sanskrit Academy, Osmania University.

Tripathi, Bh. P. (ed.). 1979. *Vākyapadīyam Part III. Vol. II, with the commentary Prakāśa by Helārāja and Ambākartrī by Raghunātha Śarmā*. Varanasi: Sampurnananda Sanskrit Vishvidyalaya.

Vasu, S. C. (ed.). 1907. वैयाकरणसिद्धान्तकौमुदी vol. I. Delhi: Motilal Banarasidas.

घिल्डियाल, श्रीधरानंद. 1977. वैयाकरणसिद्धान्तकौमुदी (हिन्दी व्याख्या सहिता) (kāraka प्रकरण). दिल्ली: मोतीलाल बनारसीदास.

त्रिपाठी, जयशंकरलाल and सुधाकर मालवीय. 1986 काशिका न्यास-Padamañjarī-भावबोधिनीसहिता vol. II. वाराणसी: तारा बुक एजन्सी.

Anita M. Borghero
Compounds at the limit:
the case of numerals in the *Aṣṭādhyāyī*

ABSTRACT

In the light of A. 6.2.35, in a research about the development of copulative compounds in the *Ṛgveda*, Ditrich (2016) writes that cardinal numerals from 'eleven' to 'nineteen' form compounds of the *dvandva* type, in which the second constituent *daśa* is in the thematic state, while the first constituent can represent all the grammatical numbers, i. e. dual *ékā-*, *dvā-*, plural *tráyo-*, singular *cátur-* and *náva-*. Whitney (1879: 183), on his side, underlines the adjectival nature of these formations.

In the slippery ground of ambiguous readings such as vt. 17 *ad* A. 2.2.29 (which proposes to include the numeral compounds among the *karmadhāraya*), the aim of this paper is to discuss the process of derivation of numeral compounds according to Pāṇini's rules, with the support of textual data collected from Vedic literature.

REFERENCES

Sharma, R. N. (ed.). 1987–2003. *The Aṣṭādhyāyī of Pāṇini*. New Delhi: MM.

Ditrich, T. 2016. "Historical development and typology of *dvandva* compounds in the *Ṛgveda*", in: J. P. Brereton (ed.), *The Vedas in Indian Culture and History: Proceedings from the Fourth International Vedic Workshop (Austin, Texas, 2007)*, pp. 75–92. Firenze: Società Editrice Fiorentina.

Whitney, W. D. 1879. *A Sanskrit grammar; including both the classical language, and the older dialects, of Veda and Brahmana*. Leipzig: Breitkopf and Härtel.

Adam A. Catt
Pāṇini's approach to verbal governing compounds with a first member in *-m*

ABSTRACT

In his paper on nominal compounds in Indo-European, Schindler (1997: 537–538) remarks that accusative case marking of the first member is obligatory in the *Ṛgveda* in certain verbal governing compounds with the suffix *-a-* whose final member is based not on the root but on the verbal stem, i. e. compounds of the type *agnim-indh-á-* '(a priest) who kindles the fire'.

Tucker (2012: 241) also notes that the consistent root vocalism *-a-* in the second member of compounds such as *vājaṃ-bhará-* 'bringing booty' (also with an accusative-marked first member) corresponds with that of the thematic present (in this case *bhárati*), suggesting that many of the compounds of this type may have a deverbative character.

In this talk, I will discuss how Pāṇini's grammar approaches this problem of the correlation between the form of the second member and a first member in *-m*.

REFERENCES

Schindler, J. 1997. "Zur internen Syntax der indogermanischen Nominalkomposita", in E. Crespo & J. L. García Ramón (eds.), *Berthold Delbrück y la sintaxis indoeuropea hoy*, pp. 537–540. Madrid: Reichert.

Tucker, E. 2012. "Brugmann's Law: The Problem of Indo-Iranian Thematic Nouns and Adjectives", in Ph. Probert & A. Willi (eds.), *Laws and Rules in Indo-European*, pp. 229–259. Oxford: Clarendon Press.

Valentina Ferrero
Is *Śī* to be considered as *anekāl* or as *śit* according to *Aṣṭhādhyāyī* 1.1.55?

ABSTRACT

As is well-known, the *Aṣṭhādhyāyī* of Pāṇini introduces Sanskrit pronouns with the rule A. 1.1.27 *sarvādīni sarvanāmani* "the word-forms beginning with *sarva* 'all' are designated as *sarvanāman* 'pronouns'". With this enumerative aphorism, Pāṇini refers to the list presented by the *Gaṇapāṭha*: (1) *sarva* 'all', (2) *viśva* 'all', (3) *ubha* 'two', (4) *ubhaya* 'both', (5) word-forms ending with the affix *Ḍatara*, (6) word-forms ending with the affix *Ḍatama*, (7) *itara* 'other', (8) *anya* 'other', (9) *anyatara* 'either', (10) *tvat* 'other', (11) *tva* 'other', (12) *nema* 'half', (13) *sama* 'all', (14) *sima* 'whole', (15) *pūrva* 'east or prior', (16) *para* 'subsequent', (17) *avara* 'west or posterior', (18) *dakṣiṇa* 'south or right', (19) *uttara* 'north or inferior, subsequent', (20) *apara* 'other or inferior', (21) *adhara* 'west or inferior', (22) *sva* 'own', (23) *antara* 'outer or an under or lower garment', (24) *tyad* 'he, she, it', (25) *tad* 'he, she, it', (26) *yad* 'who', (27) *etad* 'this', (28) *idam* 'it', (29) *adas* 'that', (30) *eka* 'one', (31) *dvi* 'two', (32) *yuṣmad* 'you', (33) *asmad* 'we', (34) *bhavat* 'you', (35) *kim* 'what'.

Considering *sarva* 'all', *viśva* 'all' and the other *sarvanāmans* ending in vowel, it is taught that the inflection of Sanskrit pronouns is *rāmavat* ('like that of Rāma') for most of the *vibhaktis*. Nevertheless, there are some points where this declension is partially different, as shown below:

Case	Singular	Dual	Plural
NOM	*sarvaḥ*	*sarvau*	*sarve* (A 7.1.17)
ACC	*sarvam*	*sarvau*	*sarvān*
INST	*sarveṇa*	*sarvābhyām*	*sarvaiḥ*
DAT	*sarvasmai* (A 7.1.14)	*sarvābhyām*	*sarvebhyaḥ*
ABL	*sarvasmāt* (A 7.1.15)	*sarvābhyām*	*sarvebhyaḥ*
GEN	*sarvasya*	*sarvayoḥ*	*sarveṣām* (A 7.1.52)
LOC	*sarvasmin* (A 7.1.15)	*sarvayoḥ*	*sarveṣu*

In the NOM string, *sarvaḥ* (*sarva* + *sU*) and *sarvau* (*sarva* + *au*) are inflected like *Rāma* (*rāmaḥ* > *rāma* + *sU*, *rāmau* > *rāma* + *au*), but at the beginning of the seventh chapter of his work, Pāṇini introduces a new aphorism in order to present the nominative masculine plural, *sarva* + *Jas*:

(1)   A 7.1.17 [*ataḥ* 9 *sarvanāmnaḥ* 14] *jasaḥ śī*
      "[After a pronominal stem ending in the short vowel *a*] *Śī* in the place of *Jas*".
      Thus, *sarva* + *Jas* > *sarva* + *Śī* > *sarve*

The word-form *sarva* 'all' is used as an example for all the masculine pronouns ending in vowel. However, what is noteworthy here is the use of this affix *Śī* and its treatment as substitute of *Jas*, according to the subsequent commentaries of the *Aṣṭhādhyāyī*.

The first and most important commentary of the grammatical tradition, i. e. the *Mahābhāṣya*, does not comment this rule.

The *Kāśikāvṛtti* instead paraphrases the *sūtra* and give some examples of its application, such as *sarve* (*sarva* + *Śī*), *viśve* (*viśva* + *Śī*), *ye* (*yad* + *Śī*), *ke* (*kim* + *Śī*), *te* (*tad* + *Śī*). Nevertheless, all the other commentaries use two different methods to explain the substitute *Śī*, according to A. 1.1.55 *anekāl śit sarvasya* 'a substitute consisting of more than one phoneme (*aL*), and a substitute having *Ś* as *IT* take the place of the whole substituend (exhibited in the sixth case)'.

On the one hand, the *Rūpāvatāra* and the *Prakriyākaumudī* teach that *Śī* replaces the whole *Jas* because the letter *Ś* of *Śī* is an *IT*. The Sanskrit text and a translation of these two works follow.

(2)   *Rupāvatāra*:
      śakāras sarvādeśārthaḥ ananekāltvāt | guṇaḥ; sarve |
      "The letter *Ś* has the meaning/aim of a total replacement [of Jas], because it does not consist of more than one phoneme. [According to the rule A. 6.1.87,] *guṇaḥ*; *sarve* (nom. pl.)".

(3)   *Prakriyākaumudī*:
      śa it | sarve |
      "*Śa* will be *it*. *sarve* (nom. pl.)".

On the other hand, all the *kaumudīs* beginning with the *Siddhāntakaumudī* by Bhaṭṭoji Dīkṣita believe that *Śī* is an affix with more than one phoneme and so it takes the place of the entire *Jas*.

(4)   *Siddhāntakaumudī*:
      anekāltvāt sarvādeśaḥ | sarvādeśatvāt prāg itsaṃjñāyāṃ evābhāvāt | sarve |

"[The substitute *Śī* has the meaning/aim of] a total replacement [of *Jas*], because it consists of more than one phoneme. Before the total replacement [of *Jas* by the substitute *Śī*, the letter *Ś*] cannot be designated as *IT. sarve* (nom. pl.)".

(5) *Madhyasiddhāntakaumudī*:
anekāltvāt sarvādeśaḥ | sarve |
"[The substitute *Śī* has the meaning/aim of] a total replacement [of *Jas*], because it consists of more than one phoneme. *sarve* (nom. pl.)".

(6) *Laghusiddhāntakaumudī*:
anekāltvāt sarvādeśaḥ | sarve |
"[The substitute *Śī* has the meaning/aim of] a total replacement [of *Jas*], because it consists of more than one phoneme. *sarve* (nom. pl.)".

(7) *Sārasiddhāntakaumudī*:
sarve |
"*sarve* (nom. pl.)".

It is evident that after a few centuries the perspective about this affixation has changed and it is now quite the opposite. This change of perspective outlines two different ways of operating among the commentaries, the *Rūpāvatāra* and the *Prakriyākaumudī* against all the other *kaumudī*s.

The *Siddhāntakaumudī* is probably the first commentary defining the substitute *Śī* as *anekāl* 'consisting of more than one phoneme'. The turning point is its reasoning in the field of *prakriyā*, because *navya vyākaraṇa* commentaries give great importance to the derivation of words. It seems that before the total replacement of *Jas* by the substitute *Śī*, the *Ś* of *Śī* cannot be defined as *IT*. However, it is possible to read the explanation of this substitution in the *Bālasiddhāntakaumudī*, that has been here divided into different passages in order to better understand the main points:

(8) *anekāltvāt sarvādeśaḥ* [Sanskrit]
anekāla hone se śī ādeśa sampūrṇā jas ke sthāna mem hotā hai sarva śī | [Hindi]
"As the substitute *Śī* consists of more than one phoneme, it takes the place of the whole *Jas*. Thus, *sarva* + *Śī* (nom. pl.)".

(9) *sthānivadbhāva se śī mem pratyaya dharma mānakara laśakvataddhite se śakāra kī itsamjñā |*

"In agreement with *sthānivadādeśo 'nalvidhau* (A 1.1.56), *Śī* has the property of being a *pratyaya*; while as stated by *laśakv ataddhite* (A 1.3.8), the technical term *IT* denotes *śa*".

(10) *tasya lopaḥ se usakā lopa sarva ī* |

"According to *tasya lopaḥ* (A 1.3.9), *lopa* replaces that (*Ś*). Thus, *sarva + ī*".

(11) *guṇaḥ* | *sarve* |

"(The sandhi is governed by the rule) *ādguṇaḥ* (A 6.1.87). Thus, *sarve*".

According to the *kaumudīs*, *Śī* can receive the definition of *pratyaya* only via *stānivadbhāva*. That is, on account of its being a replacement of the affix *Jas*. Assignment of the term *pratyaya* facilitates assignment of the term *IT* to *Ś* by A 1.3.8 *laśakv ataddhite*. This, in turn, facilitates deletion of *Ś* by A 1.3.9 *tasya lopaḥ*. For this reason, a total replacement of *Jas* by *Śī* is not accomplished because of *Ś* as an *IT*. It is, instead, accomplished on the basis of its *anekāltva* '(the affix *Śī*) consists of more than one phoneme'.

It is clear that Bhaṭṭojī Dīkṣita presents this new way of operating among different rules as something already established. For this reason, it would be really interesting to better understand when and above all why this perspective has changed. Therefore, the presentation will introduce the substitute *Śī* and the problem of its definition, but then it will also consider the commentaries between the *Prakriyākaumudī* (14th–15th century) and the *Siddhāntakaumudī* (16th–17th centuries). In fact, the principal aim of this project will be a deep investigation in the reasoning of these works: the focus will be trying to establish the turning point in the *unekāl-śit* question that has inspired Bhaṭṭojī Dīkṣita and all the following *kaumudīs* until nowadays.

BIBLIOGRAPHY

Devasthali, G. V. (ed.). 1968. *Sārasiddhāntakaumudī of Varadarāja, edited with introduction, translation, and critical and exegetical notes*. Poona: Centre of Advanced Study in Sanskrit.

Joshi, S. Ś., and R. C. Jhā (eds.). 1960. *Śrīvaradarājācāryaviracitā madhyasiddhāntakaumudī sudhā indumatī saṃskṛtahindivyākhyopetā*. Varanasi: Chowkhamba.

Kanshi, R. (ed.). 2010–2012. *The Laghusiddhāntakaumudī of Varadarāja, a primer of Pāṇini's grammar*. Delhi: Motilal Banarsidass.

Kielhorn, F. (ed.). 1880–1885. *The Vyâkarana-Mahâbhâshya of Patanjali*. Bombay: Government Central Book Depôt.

Miśra, J. S. (ed.). 1991. *Bālasiddhāntakaumudī*. Vārāṇasī: Viśvavidyālaya Prakāśana.

Rangacharya, M., and M. B. Varadarajiengar (eds.). 1916–1927. *The Rūpāvatāra of Dharmakīrti, with additions and emendations for the use of college students.* Madras: Natesan; Bangalore: The Bangalore Press.

Sharma, A., K. Deshpande, and D. G. Padhye (eds.). 1969–1970. *Kāśikā, a commentary on Panini's grammar by Vāmana and Jayāditya.* Hyderabad: Sanskrit Academy, Osmania University.

Trivedi, K. P. (ed.). 1925–1931. *The Prakriyākaumudī of Rāmachandra (in two parts) with the commentary Prasāda of Viṭṭhala and with a critical notice of manuscripts and an exhaustive and critical introduction.* Poona: Bhandarkar Oriental Research Institute.

Vasu, S. C. (ed.). 1905–1907. *The Siddhānta Kaumudī of Bhaṭṭoji Dīkṣita, edited and translated into English.* Allahabad: Panini Office.

Artemij Keidan
Hiding a verb: ritual vs. courtly interpretation
of *Aṣṭhādhyāyī* 1.4.34

ABSTRACT

In the present paper, I am dealing with the meaning of the grammatical rule
prescribed in Pāṇini's *sutra* 1.4.34 that belongs to the subsection describing the
sampradāna, i.e. the *kāraka* role corresponding to the 'recipient' of an action.
This is a simplified translation of the *sūtra*:

(1) *ślāgha-hnuṅ-sthā-śapāñ jñīpsyamānaḥ*
   "With the verbs *ślāgh* 'to praise', *hnu* 'to hide', *sthā* 'to make a statement',
   śap 'to swear', the person to whom the communication is delivered is to be
   classified as «recipient»".

Here, the *sampradānu* is described as *jñīpsyamānaḥ*. This tricky term is a pas-
sive present participle from a desiderative constructed upon a causative derived
from the verb *jñā* 'to know'. Therefore, it literally means 'the person whom someone wants to be caused to know'. Or, more freely, 'the addressee of speaking'.

Indeed, three of the four verbs quoted in the rule describe activities falling
into the scope of speaking. The roots *ślāgh* and *śap* are self-explaining in such
respect. The root *sthā* is less obvious: it literally means 'to stand', but here is
apparently used in the metaphoric sense of 'putting forward a proposition', or
'making a statement' (to use a western term that is likewise derived from the
root of 'standing' but is used as a verb of speaking).

Only *hnu* stands out from this series: there is no simple way for connecting
'hiding' to 'speaking'. Thus, my main goal is to explain this apparent inconsistency, more specifically: the reason why the verb *hnu* appears in a collection of
verba dicendi?

Pāṇinīya tradition is of little help in answering this question. Patañjali does
not comment on this *sūtra*. Later commentators seem confused about its real
meaning (cf. Palsule 1987: 657, fn. 8). Haradatta (commenting on the *Kāśikāvṛtti*)

even admits that there may be two different readings here. From the *Kāśikāvṛtti* onwards, Pāṇini's commentators and illustrators are mainly concerned with the explanation of the meaning of *jñīpsyamāna* referred to the *sampradāna* in connection with the four verbs of this rule. Particularly with *hnu*, the commentators sought to accommodate the idea of 'hiding from someone' with the idea of 'making this same person know about such hiding', which is an obvious contradiction. As a result, almost all of the examples suggested by the commentators on this regard describe scenes of deliberate ambiguity, such as, for example, a situation in which a person tries to deceive the creditors, or, again, a love intrigue, in which someone *pretends* to hide from her/his partner only in order to attract his/her attention. Only the playfulness of flirting could justify such a contradiction (cf. Catullus' *odi et amo* 'I hate and I love').

Grammatically, the dative-marked complement (the *sampradāna*) is usually considered the person *from whom* something is being hidden, as in (2):

(2) a. *Kṛṣṇāya hnute iti. Sapatnyapanayanena svāśayaṃ kṛṣṇaṃ bodhayati.*
"An example for *hnute* 'she hides from Kṛṣṇa' goes as follows. By removing herself from the fellow-wives, she reveals to Kṛṣṇa her desire" (*Bālamanoramā* on *Siddhāntakaumudī* 572).

   b. *...nihnuvāno 'sau Sītāyai*
"...he [=Rāvaṇa], who disguises his true nature from Sītā" (*Bhaṭṭikāvya* 8.74; cf. Kawamura 2018: 68, 2nd interpretation).

The second reading of these examples, mentioned by Haradatta (in his *Padamañjari*, a commentary on the *Kāśikāvṛtti*), considers *hnu* a transitive verb with an odd dative-marked direct object. Moreover, this object of hiding is identified with the addressee of the action. See the examples in (3):

(3) a. *Sapatnībhyaḥ kṛṣṇaṃ hnuvānā tamevārthaṃ kṛṣṇaṃ bodhayati.*
"While hiding Kṛṣṇa from the fellow-wives, she reveals this fact to Kṛṣṇa" (*Tattvabodhinī* 508).

   b. *...nihnuvāno 'sau Sītāyai*
"...he [=Rāvaṇa], who conceals Sītā [from the demons]" (*Bhaṭṭikāvya* 8.74; cf. Kawamura 2018: 68, 1st interpretation).

   c. *Devadattāya hnute iti. Sannihitam eva Devadattaṃ dhanikāder apalapatīty arthaḥ.*
"The meaning of *Devadattāya hnute* 'He conceals to Devadatta' goes as follows. Someone hides Devadatta just in front of him from the creditor and the like" (*Padamañjari* on *Kāśikāvṛtti* on 1.4.34).

This "pseudo-transitive" interpretation of *hnu* is found in some modern editions of the *Aṣṭādhyāyī* (e.g. Katre 1987: 85), while others (e.g. Joshi & Roodbergen 1995: 108) do not even mention it. Importantly, there seem to be no examples of the "pseudo-transitive" construction in the Vedic corpus (De-Schai Olsen 2012: 28).

In my opinion, another solution is possible, one that will demystify the "mystery of *hnu*" in the rule 1.4.34. It consists in the following steps.

1. The term *jñīpsyamāna* should be "degrammaticalized". If we read it as a simple noun (meaning 'addressee'), rather than a highly complex deverbal formation, there would be no need to justify the 'intentionality' codified by the desiderative.

2. The verb *hnu* should be read as a verb of speaking. This is supported by a number of sources. In the *Vedas* the root *hnu*, always prefixed, is used to express the action of repentance. In the *Amarakośa* (1.6.17.1) this root is glossed as a synonym of *apalāpa* 'denial', which might be the source of Haradatta (see ex. 3c). Therefore, *hnu* primarily means 'concealing something' (e.g. the sins during the ritual of repentance) through the force of words, rather than by a physical removal.

3. The misunderstanding of the semantics of *hnu* might be explained by imagining a gradual secularization of Pāṇini's grammar. The grammar was born in Antiquity as a ritual-related *Vedāṅga*. On the contrary, during the Middle Ages it evolved into a matter of lay culture, patronized by aristocrats and kings. Accordingly, the universe of the discourse of the grammar changed from a religious one to that of the courtly culture.

REFERENCES

Joshi, Sh. D., and J. A. F. Roodbergen (ed.). 1995. *The Aṣṭādhyāyī of Pāṇini with translation and explanatory notes. Vol. IV (1.4.1–1.4.110)*. New Delhi: Sahitya Akademi.

Katre, S. M. 1987. *Aṣṭādhyāyī of Pāṇini. Roman transliteration and English translation*. Austin: University of Texas Press.

Kawamura, Y. 2018. *The kāraka theory embodied in the Rāma story. A Sanskrit textbook in Medieval India*. New Delhi: DK Printworld.

Palsule, G. B. 1987. "*Tādarthye caturthī* vis-à-vis Pāṇini's treatment of the kārakas and the dative", *Annals of the Bhandarkar Oriental Research Institute* 68: 653–659.

Ramanathan, A. A. (ed.). 1971–1995. *Amarakośa, with the unpublished South Indian commentaries*. Madras: The Adayar library and Research center.

De-Schai Olsen, J. 2012. *The Dative in Ṛgvedic Sanskrit*. Master's thesis, University of Oslo.

Andrey Klebanov
On the meaning of the term *prakaraṇa* in the earliest texts of the Pāṇinian system of Sanskrit grammar

ABSTRACT

In my talk, I will present a short lexicographic study that concentrates on various aspects of meaning given to the term *prakaraṇa* in the early texts of the Pāṇinian system, from Kātyāyana's *vārttika*s to the works of Bhartṛhari. Though in no way central to the Pāṇinian system, this term attracted my attention for two reasons.

Firstly, it belongs to a basic technical vocabulary employed for the analysis of linguistic expressions by scholars of different *śāstra*s. Hence, improving our understanding of the term in one field of knowledge may help us appreciate its use in other fields.

Secondly, I will demonstrate that the meaning of the term *prakaraṇa* underwent a certain shift within the Pāṇinian system itself: from (1) a technical concept pertaining to the working of the *Aṣṭādhyāyī* in Kātyāyana's terminology to (2) a broader notion belonging to the field akin to the discourse analysis in Bhartṛhari's parlance.

It is the second meaning that became prominent and, from ca. 9th cent. onward was adopted, for example, in the newly emergent field of Sanskrit aesthetics (*alaṃkāraśāstra*). Within this system, it provided the basis for one of the fundamental taxonomies (*prākaraṇika-aprākaraṇika*) commonly applied to the analysis of poetic utterances. It is employed in order to distinguish between elements of content that are, on the one side of the spectrum, directly related to the "actual" scene described in the poem, to the topic at hand, the main plot etc., and on the other side, to what is excluded from the above field, namely, elements that are not directly related to the current description, scene, plot etc. Loosely translated then, the term *prākaraṇika* refers to the senses which are 'contextually relevant', and *aprākaraṇika* to reciprocal senses that are 'contextually irrelevant', or 'non-contextual', while the headword *prakaraṇa* is usually rendered as 'context'.

The latter translation is also commonly employed in rendering the term *prakaraṇa* in technical works of *vyākaraṇa* and *mīmāṃsā*, where the *śāstras* allow a more precise understanding. In Bhartṛhari's *oeuvre*, to be specific, *prakaraṇa* is often paired with a related term *artha*. Based on (partly corrupt, yet unambiguous) glosses found in the ancient *Vṛtti* as well as in Puṇyarāja's *Ṭīkā* (ca. 10th century) on *Vākyapadīya* 2.314 and 2.315–317, we learn that *artha* designates what modern scholarship calls 'co-text' — that is, the immediate linguistic environment of the analysed expression — while *prakaraṇa* refers to the 'context' proper — that is, the non-linguistic environment. In the sentence *saindhavam ānaya!* "Fetch *saindhava*!", when it is used in a direct linguistic environment of another sentence *mṛgayāṃ kariṣyāmi* 'I will go hunting', *artha* allows to understand that the word *saindhava* refers to a 'horse'. When, however, the same sentence is uttered while setting up a dining table without anything else being said, *prakaraṇa* allows comprehending *saindhava* as referring to 'salt'. In accordance with this finding, it seems likely that the compound *arthaprakaraṇa* often employed by Bhartṛhari should be interpreted as a *dvandva*, although several modern scholars suggested understanding it as a Genitive *tatpuruṣa*. In my talk, I will present the above definitions of *artha* and *prakaraṇa* and briefly consider several usages of the compound *arthaparakaraṇa* to test the hypothesis about its analysis.

Another essential source for tacking the semantics of *prakaraṇa* are texts of the *mīmāṃsāśāstra*. Within this system, *prakaraṇa* is given the status of an important technical term employed to interpret Vedic statements. Its various applications have been discussed in several recent papers and are not directly relevant for our purpose (see McCrea 2000; Yoshimizu 2006; 2011; Cardona 2013).

In my talk, I will briefly look at Śabara's definition of *prakaraṇa* (given in the commentary on MīSū 3.3.14), according to which *prakaraṇa* is taken quite literally to refer to a statement that was made prior to the one being currently considered.

The sense of the term *prakaraṇa* thus identified in the *Mīmāṃsāsūtrabhāṣya* resonates exceptionally well with its attestations in Kātyāyana's *vārttikas*, where it occurs for more than 80 times. As I will demonstrate in my talk, some of these usages along with their unpacking in the *Mahābhāṣya* provide a strong argument for thinking that Kātyāyana used *prakaraṇa* as a quasi-synonym of the term *anuvṛtti*. For him, to say that an "element X is *prakṛta*", or that there is "*prakaraṇa* of X" seems synonymous with stating that "X *anuvartate*", or that there is "*anuvṛtti* of X" respectively.

After establishing this hypothesis about the meaning of *prakaraṇa*, I will look at a selection of less conclusive textual instances in order to test my assumption. I will argue that even if it is possible, after all, to translate *prakaraṇa* as 'context' (in a non-technical sense of the word), understanding it as a synonym of *anuvṛtti* allows more precise comprehension of Kātyāyana's arguments.

REFERENCES

McCrea, L. 2000. "The hierarchical organization of language in mīmāmsā interpretive theory", *Journal of Indian Philosophy* 28.5–6: 429–459.

Yoshimizu, K. 2006. "The theorem of the singleness of a goblet (*graha-ekatva-nyāya*). A *mīmāṃsā* analysis of meaning and context", *Acta Asiatica* 90: 15–38.

Yoshimizu, K. 2011. "How to refer to a thing by a word: another difference between Dignāga's and Kumārila's theories of denotation", *Journal of Indian Philosophy* 39.4–5: 571–587.

Cardona, G. 2013. "Mīmāṃsā and the Pāṇinian system", *Annals of the Bhandarkar Oriental Research Institute* 94: 7–110.

Davide Mocci
The *sāmānādhikaraṇya* relation and the *upasarjana*: insights from Pāṇini and the Generative Grammar

INTRODUCTION

In accordance with the Indian grammatical tradition, every compound can be solved into a combination of nominal *pada*s (i.e., fully inflected words) P_1 and P_2 such that the Case-ending of P_1 and that of P_2 are overtly realized. This combination is referred to as *vigraha* or constituent analysis of the compound. Thus, the *vigraha* of the *tatpuruṣa* compound *aśva-śapha-* 'horse's hoof' (ŚB 1.2.2.10b) is the combination NP* of *aśva-sya* 'horse-GEN' with an inflected form of *śapha-* 'hoof'. NP* may be embedded within different sentences, as illustrated in (1).

(1) a. *asti* [$_{NP^*}$ *aśvasya   śaphaḥ*].
       is   horse-GEN   hoof-NOM
       "A horse's hoof exists".

    b. [$_{NP^*}$ *aśvasya   śapham*]   *paśyāmi*.
       horse-GEN   hoof-ACC   see-IND.PRS.3SG
       "I see a horse's hoof"

    c. [$_{NP^*}$ *śaphāt aśvasya*]   *śatam*   *kumbhān asiñcatam   madhūnām*.
       hoof-ABL   horse-GEN   hundred-ACC   pots-ACC   you_poured honey-GEN
       "You poured a hundred pots of honey from the horse's hoof" (ṚV 1.117.6b).

Interestingly, the Case-ending of *aśva-* remains unchanged in (1) (*aśva-* is inflected in the genitive in (1a) through (1c)), although NP* fulfills different syntactic functions in (1): NP* is the subject in (1a), the direct object in (1b), and the complement of origin in (1c). By contrast, the Case-ending of *śapha-* changes according to the syntactic function fulfilled by NP* in each of these three sentences. Now, in A. 1.2.44 Pāṇini defines the *upasarjana* as the nominal *pada* that is *ekavibhakti*, lit. 'whose Case-ending remains one' in a compound. According to the reading of A. 1.2.44 advanced by Pontillo (2003: 22), for a nominal *pada* P to be *ekavibhakti* in a compound C means that the Case-ending of P remains unchanged in the *vigraha* XP of C regardless of the syntactic function fulfilled by XP in the sentence. Since the Case-ending of *aśva-* remains unchanged in the NP* of (1), *aśva-* satisfies the condition of being *ekavibhakti* taught by A. 1.2.44. Therefore, *aśva-* qualifies as *upasarjana* in compliance with A. 1.2.44. That *aśva-* is *upasarjana* in the NP* of (1) is confirmed by the following observation.

A. 2.2.8 teaches that a *ṣaṣṭhī* (i.e., a nominal *pada* inflected in the genitive) combines with a nominal *pada* to form a *tatpuruṣa* compound. *Ṣaṣṭhī* is mentioned in the nominative in A. 2.2.8, which is a rule devoted to the formation of compounds. A. 1.2.43 provides that, in the rules devoted to the formation of compounds (A. 2.1.2), the use of the nominative for mentioning a certain expression X is a metalinguistic device that serves to identify (the linguistic forms falling under the scope of) X as *upasarjana*. The *aśva-* contained in the NP* of (1) falls under the scope of *ṣaṣṭhī* (A 2.2.8) on a par with the *aśva-* of *aśva-śapha-*; hence, A. 2.2.8 identifies both the *aśva-* of *aśva-śapha-* and the *aśva-* contained in the NP* of (1) as *upasarjana*. See Candotti and Pontillo (2019: 22–24) for discussion.

Consider now the *karmadhāraya* compound *eka-vīra-* 'unique hero' (ṚV 10.103.1b). *Eka-* conveys the meaning 'one', and *vīra-* conveys the meaning 'hero' in *eka-vīra-*. Both these meanings may be conceived as properties that fall upon (or are ascribed to) an entity x. For instance, the property of being one (corresponding to the meaning of *eka-*) and the property of being a hero (corresponding to the meaning of *vīra-*) both fall upon the same entity 'Indra' in the Ṛgvedic passage quoted above. In Pāṇini's grammar, if the property corresponding to the meaning of a pada P_1 and the property corresponding to the meaning of another pada P_2 fall upon one and the same entity x, P_1 is said to be *samānādhikaraṇa* with P_2 (*samānādhikaraṇa* literally means 'having the same substratum' and is translated as 'coreferential' by Cardona 1997: 217; cf. Kiparsky 2009: 54). Therefore, *eka-* is *samānādhikaraṇa* with *vīra-* in *eka-vīra-*. Now, *eka-vīra-* is governed by A. 2.1.49, stating that *eka-* combines with a nominal *pada* which is *samānādhikaraṇa* with *eka-* to form a *karmadhāraya* compound. *Eka-* is mentioned in the nominative in A. 2.1.49 (more precisely, *eka-* is contained within the long compound *pūrvakālaikasarvajaratpurāṇanavakevala-*, which is mentioned in the nominative in this rule). As a consequence, the expressions falling under the scope of the *eka-* of A. 2.1.49 qualify as *upasarjana*. Since the *eka-* of *eka-vīra-* falls under the scope of the *eka-* of A. 2.1.49, the *eka-* of *eka-vīra-* is *upasarjana*.

Things get interesting when the *vigraha* of *eka-vīra-* is considered. The *vigraha* of *eka-vīra-* is the combination NP of *eka-* with *vīra-* such that *eka-* agrees in Case with *vīra-* in NP. By embedding NP within different sentences, we obtain (2).

(2) a. *asti* [$_{NP}$ *ekaḥ   vīraḥ*].
    is   unique-NOM hero-NOM
    "There is a unique hero".

   b. [$_{NP}$ *ekam   vīram*]   *paśyāmi.*
     one-ACC hero-ACC see-IND.PRS.3SG
     "I see a unique hero".

   c. [$_{NP}$ *ekāya   vīrāya*]   *vājam   yacchāmi.*
     one-DAT hero-DAT award-ACC confer-IND.PRS.1SG
     "I am conferring the award to a unique hero".

Both the Case-ending of *eka-* and that of *vīra-* change when the syntactic function fulfilled by NP changes in (2): both *eka-* and *vīra-* are inflected in the nominative in (2a) (i.e., when NP is the subject), in the accusative in (2b) (i.e., when the NP is the direct object), and in the dative in (2c) (i.e., when NP is the indirect object). In brief, *eka-* agrees in Case with *vīra-* in (2). Indeed, the Case-agreement between *eka-* and *vīra-* in (2) is a consequence of the *sāmānādhikaraṇya* 'coreferentiality' relation holding between *eka-* and *vīra-* in (2): in fact, Case-agreement systematically correlates with the *sāmānādhikaraṇya* relation.

Now, neither *eka-* nor *vīra-* satisfies the condition of being *ekavibhakti* (taught by A. 1.2.44) in the NP of (2), i.e., in the *vigraha* of *eka-vīra-*. Therefore, both *eka-* and *vīra-* qualify as non-*upasarjana* in the NP of (2) in accordance with A. 1.2.44. However, the *eka-* contained in the NP of (2) falls under the scope of the *eka-* mentioned in the nominative in A. 2.1.49: this implies that the *eka-* contained in the NP of (2) is *upasarjana* on a par with the *eka-* of *eka-vīra-*. We have then run into a contradiction: *eka-* in the NP of (2) should count as non-*upasarjana* in accordance with A. 1.2.44 but should count as *upasarjana* in accordance with A. 2.1.49. The same problem indeed emerges in the *vigraha* of every compound governed by A. 2.1.49, i.e., in the vigraha of every *karmadhāraya*: this is because, in the *vigraha* of every compound governed by A. 2.1.49, one *pada* is *upasarjana* but at the same time *samānādhikaraṇa* (hence, in Case-agreement) with another *pada*.

This study addresses the following research question: is there a way to avoid the contradiction into which we have run in (2)? In other words, is the notion *upasarjana* as defined in A. 1.2.44 compatible with the *sāmānādhikaraṇya* relation? We shall review some evidence internal to the *Aṣṭādhyāyī* which points towards an affirmative answer. Next, we shall translate the solution to this problem into formal terms, by capitalizing on the tree notation developed within the generative framework. This formalization is helpful in two senses: on the one hand, it helps us better understand the aforementioned solution; on the other hand, it provides a more general linguistic basis to such a solution.

The term *samānādhikaraṇa* also shows up in A. 3.2.124: *laṭaḥ śatṛśānacāv aprathamāsamānādhikaraṇe*. This rule teaches that, when *LAṬ* (i.e., the placeholder standing for the verbal endings that are attached to the present tense-aspect stem) is *samānādhikaraṇa* with a *pada* inflected in a Case other than nominative, then *LAṬ* must be replaced by the participial suffix *-nt-* or *-(m)āna-*, rather than by a finite verbal ending (e.g., the 3sg ending *-ti*) (Sharma 2002: 427; Lowe 2015: 331, 334–335). E.g., *devadatta-* is inflected in the nominative and *LAṬ* is *samānādhikaraṇa* with *devadatta-* in (3a): to wit, the property of being an agent (which corresponds to the meaning of *LAṬ* in accordance with A. 3.4.69) and the property of being Devadatta (which corresponds to the meaning of *devadatta-*) both fall upon the same entity x (i.e., the entity called 'Devadatta'). As a result, the replacement of *LAṬ* by the 3sg ending *-ti* is possible, as in (3b); put another way, the replacement of *LAṬ* by *-nt-*, as in (3c) is not compulsory. Conversely, *devadatta-* is inflected in the accusative and *LAṬ* is *samānādhikaraṇa* with *devadatta-* in (4a). Therefore, *LAṬ* can be replaced by *-nt-* but not by *-ti*: see the contrast between (4b) and (4c) (for this argument see Sharma 2002: 428).

(3) a. *devadattaḥ   odanam   paca-LAṬ.*
     Devadatta-NOM   rise-ACC   cook-*LAṬ*

   b. *devadattaḥ   odanam   pacati.*
     Devadatta-NOM   rise-ACC   cook-IND.PRS.3SG
     "Devadatta is cooking rice".

   c. *devadattaḥ   odanam   pacān.*
     Devadatta-NOM   rise-ACC   cook-PRS.PTCP.NOM
     "Devadatta, who is cooking rice".

(4) a. *aham   odanam   paca-LAṬ'   devadattam   paśyāmi.*
     I   rise-ACC   cook-*LAṬ*   Devadatta-ACC   see-IND.PRS.1SG

   b. **aham   odanam   pacati   devadattam   paśyāmi.*
     I   rise-ACC   cook-IND.PRS.3SG   Devadatta-ACC   see-IND.PRS.1SG

   c. *aham   odanam   pacantam   devadattam   paśyāmi.*
     I   rise-ACC   cook-PRS.PTCP.ACC   Devadatta-ACC   see-IND.PRS.1SG
     "I see Devadatta cooking rise".

In short, one cannot know that *LAṬ* is to be replaced by the PRS.PTCP suffix *-nt-* rather than by the IND.PRS.3SG ending *-ti* in (4) if s/he does not first know that *devadatta-* is inflected in the accusative rather than in the nominative in this sentence. But this means that the Case-ending of *devadatta-* must be determined before and independently of the replacement of *LAṬ* by *-nt-*. This fact has dramatic consequences. Consider why.

Both *devadatta-* and *-nt-* are inflected in the accusative in (4c). Since the Case-ending of *devadatta-* is determined before (and independently of) the replacement of *LAṬ* by *-nt-* in (4c), the Case-ending of *devadatta-* must be determined before (and independently of) the Case-ending of *-nt-* too. Moreover, since *LAṬ* is *samānādhikaraṇa* with *devadatta-* in (4a) by virtue of A. 3.2.124, *-nt-*, which replaces *LAṬ* in (4c), is also *samānādhikaraṇa* with *devadatta-*. The following picture then emerges from the analysis of A. 3.2.124: the Case-ending of an element E_1 (i.e., *devadatta-*) is determined before and independently of the Case-ending of another element E_2 (i.e., *-nt-*) such that E_2 is *samānādhikaraṇa* with E_1.

Now, the accusative Case-ending of *devadatta-* in (4c) is determined by A. 2.3.2: this ending attaches to *devadatta-* in order to signify the patient (*karman*) of the action of seeing. The accusative Case-ending of *-nt-* in (4c) cannot be determined in the same manner. Indeed, if the accusative Case-ending attached to *-nt-* in (4c) in order to signify the patient of the action of seeing, the *anabhihite* constraint (which requires that whatever is signified by a nominal ending be only signified once) would be violated (A. 2.3.1, see Kiparsky 2009: 50): the patient of the action of seeing would be signified by two distinct nominal endings, namely the accusative Case-ending of *devadatta-* and the accusative Case-ending of *-nt-*. As a consequence, the Case-ending of *-nt-* must be determined in an alternative way. We submit that the accusative Case-ending of *-nt-* is determined by the operation of Case-copying: *-nt-* copies the accusative Case-ending of *devadatta-*, which was determined before and independently of the Case-ending of *-nt-*. This Case-copying is contingent upon the presence of the *sāmānādhikaraṇya* relation: in fact, the visible reflex of the fact that a pada P_1 has copied the Case-ending of another pada P_2 is that P_1 agrees in Case with P_2; but, as already said, Case-agreement systematically correlates with the *sāmānādhikaraṇya* relation; hence, Case-copying necessarily requires the *sāmānādhikaraṇya* relation. In other words, if *-nt-* were not *samānādhikaraṇa* with *devadatta-*, *-nt-* would lack a Case-ending because none of the ordinary conditions which may provide *-nt-* with a Case-ending (i.e., the conditions listed in section A. 2.3) is satisfied.

In sum, A. 3.2.124 testifies to the existence of two levels in the derivation of (4c), namely L_1 and L_2, with L_1 preceding L_2: *devadatta-* is inflected in the accusative and *-nt-* lacks a Case-ending at L_1; however, the *sāmānādhikaraṇya* relation intervenes at L_2 to provide *-nt-* with a Case-ending, by triggering the operation of Case-copying. Put another way, *-nt-* lacks a Case-ending at L_1 and acquires a Case-ending at L_2. We may identify L_1 as the derivational level at which Case-endings are determined by the rules of A. 2.3, and L_2 as the derivational level at which the *sāmānādhikaraṇya* relation is established. Let us now return to the issue of determining the *upasarjana* in (2).

The Case-ending of *vīra-* in (2) is determined by one of the rules contained in section A. 2.3: e.g., the accusative Case-ending attaches to *vīra-* in (2b) to express the patient of the action of seeing (A. 2.3.2); the dative Case-ending attaches to *vīra-* in (2c) to express the recipient (*sampradāna*) of the action of conferring (A. 2.3.13). By contrast, the Case-ending of *eka-* in (2) cannot be determined by any of the rules contained in A. 2.3. E.g., if the accusative Case-ending attached to *eka-* in (2b) in order to signify the patient of the action of seeing, the *anabhihite* constraint would be violated: the patient of the action of seeing would be signified by two distinct nominal endings, namely the accusative Case-ending of *eka-* and the accusative Case-ending of *vīra-*. We submit that *eka-* copies the Case-ending of *vīra-* in (2) by virtue of *eka-* being *samānādhikaraṇa* with *vīra-* (the *sāmānādhikaraṇya* relation between *eka-* and *vīra-* in (2) is provided for by A. 2.1.49).

Thus, we may say that two levels L_1 and L_2 (defined as above) exist in the derivation of (2) too: *vīra-* has a Case-ending at L_1 (i.e., one of the rules of A. 2.3 provides *vīra-* with a Case-ending), and *eka-* lacks a Case-ending at L_1 (i.e., none of the rules of A. 2.3 provides *eka-* with a Case-ending); yet, the *sāmānādhikaraṇya* relation intervenes at L_2 to provide *eka-* with a Case-ending, by copying the Case-ending of *vīra-* onto *eka-*. To wit, *eka-* lacks a Case-ending at L_1 and acquires a Case-ending at L_2. Now, we assume that A. 1.2.44 applies at level L_1, i.e., before the *sāmānādhikaraṇya* relation is established. But the Case-ending of *eka-* in (2) only changes by virtue of *eka-* being *samānādhikaraṇa* with *vīra-* in this sentence. Therefore, if A. 1.2.44 applies at L_1, this rule does not 'see' *eka-* getting different Case-endings (as in (2)): indeed, *eka-* has no Case-ending whatsoever at L_1. That is, the *sāmānādhikaraṇya* relation acts as a sort of disturbing factor with respect to the standard determination of Case-endings (i.e., the determination of Case-endings provided for by the rules of A. 2.3), and A. 1.2.44 abstracts away from this disturbing factor.

Two alternative scenarios open up at this point. According to the first scenario, the *eka-* in the NP of (2) simply falls outside the scope of *ekavibhakti* taught by A. 1.2.44: the *eka-* in the NP of (2) neither satisfies nor violates the condition of being *ekavibhakti*, because this condition only pertains to *padas* whose Case-ending has already been determined at L_1, while the *eka-* in the NP of (2) lacks a Case-ending at L_1. According to the second scenario, the *eka-* in the NP of (2) satisfies the condition of being *ekavibhakti* taught by A. 1.2.44: the fact that the *eka-* in the NP of (2) lacks a Case-ending at L_1 suffices for considering *eka-* on a par with those *padas* whose Case-ending remains one, and apart from those *padas* whose Case-ending changes: indeed, an absent Case-ending does not change by definition. Crucially, neither of these scenarios forces us to consider the *eka-* in the NP of (2) as non-*upasarjana*.

In conclusion, the *upasarjana*-status of the *eka-* contained in the NP of (2), warranted by A. 2.1.49, is not voided by the fact that the Case-ending of *eka-* changes in (2). Consequently, A. 2.1.49 is not in contradiction with A. 1.2.44.

FORMALIZATION

The formalism developed within the generative framework makes it possible to draw a distinction between the Case-ending of *eka-* and the Case-ending of *vīra-* in (2). Consider the phrase marker for (2b), depicted in (5) below. Here the Adjectival Phrase (AP) headed by *eka-* is contained within the Specifier of the Case-head K°_1, which in turn takes the NP *vīra-* as complement (on the representation of AP as being contained in the Specifier of a functional head that gravitates around NP, see, e.g., Cinque 2005: 317; on the representation of Case-endings as sitting under K°, see Bittner and Hale 1996). Crucially, *vīra-* is closer than *eka-* with respect to *paśyāmi* in (5): indeed, two nodes intervene between VP (i.e., the first node dominating both *vīra-* and *paśyāmi*) and *vīra-* (see (5a)), while three nodes intervene between VP (i.e., the first node dominating both *eka-* and *paśyāmi*) and *eka-* (see (5b)).

(5a)   (5b)

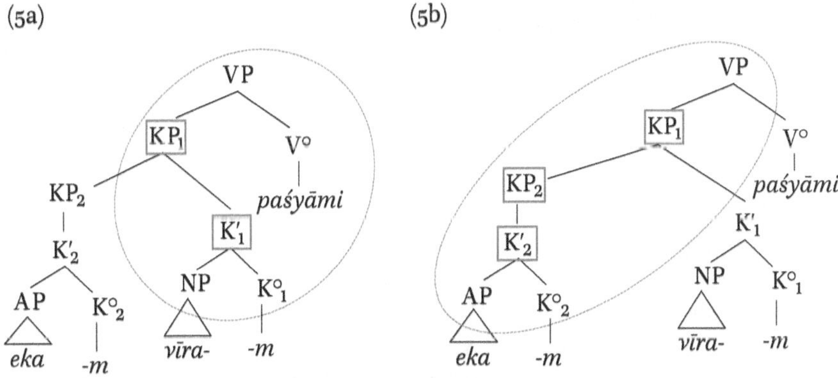

Exploiting the observation that *vīra-* is closer than *eka-* with respect to *paśyāmi*, we may say that only the accusative Case-ending of *vīra-* is determined by the influence, so to speak, of the transitive verb *paśyāmi*, and that the accusative Case-ending of *eka-* is instead the result of *eka-* copying the previously determined (accusative) Case-ending of *vīra-*. In other words, the accusative Case-ending of *eka-* cannot be directly determined by the influence of *paśyāmi*, insofar as *eka-* is too far away from *paśyāmi*. Thus, the determination of the Case-endings of *vīra-* and *eka-* is split into two different steps in (5): Step One, in which *vīra-* receives a Case-ending by virtue of being under the influence of the transitive verb *paśyāmi*, and Step Two, in which *eka-* receives a Case-ending by virtue of copying the Case-ending of *vīra-*.

By capitalizing on A. 3.2.124, we have shown that the determination of the Case-endings of *eka-* and *vīra-* in (2) is split into two different steps: first, the Case-ending of *vīra-* is determined by one of the rules of A. 2.3; second, the Case-ending of *vīra-* is copied onto *eka-* after the establishment of the *sāmānādhikaraṇya* relation between *vīra-* and *eka-*. This two-step determination of Case-endings is not a bizarre idea, insofar as it can also be translated into formal terms: see (5). What is more, the two-step determination of Case-endings makes it possible to confine the definition of *upasarjana* as the nominal *pada* "whose Case-ending remains one" (A 1.2.44) to a derivational level which precedes the establishment of the *sāmānādhikaraṇya* relation. This reconciles the notion *upasarjana* as defined in A. 1.2.44 with the *sāmānādhikaraṇya* relation, which seemed prima facie mutually incompatible.

REFERENCES

Bittner, M., and K. Hale. 1996. "The Structural Determination of Case and Agreement", *Linguistic Inquiry* 27.1: 1–68.

Candotti, M. P., and T. Pontillo. 2019. "Lexical subordination in derivation and compounding". *Studi e Saggi Linguistici* 58.2: 155–175.

Cardona, G. 1997. *Pāṇini: His Work and Its Tradition, Vol. 1: Background and Introduction*. Delhi: Motilal Banarsidass.

Cinque, G. 2005. "Deriving Greenberg's Universal 20 and Its Exceptions", *Linguistic Inquiry* 36.3: 315–332.

Kiparsky, P. 2009. "On the architecture of Pāṇini's grammar", in G. Huet, A. Kulkarni, & P. Scharf (eds.), *Sanskrit Computational Linguistics, ISCLS 2007/2008*. Lecture Notes in Computer Science 5402: 33–94.

Lowe, J. J. 2015. *Participles in Rigvedic Sanskrit: The Syntax and Semantics of Adjectival Verb Forms*. Oxford: Oxford University Press.

Pontillo, T. 2003. "La definizione di *upasarjana-* in Pāṇini", in R. Ronzitti & G. Borghi (eds.), *Atti del Primo Incontro Genovese di Studi Vedici e Pāṇiniani (Genova, 16 luglio 2002)*, 21–35. Recco: Le Mani.

Sharma, R. N. 2002. *The Aṣṭādhyāyī of Pāṇini*. Vol. 3. New Delhi: Munshiram Manoharlal.

Chiara Pette
Xuanzang's transcription of Sanskrit declension and the reconstruction of Middle Chinese phonology

The topic of this presentation is a peculiar case of Chinese characters used as phonographical device: the interesting attempt to represent the declension paradigm of Sanskrit *puruṣa* 'man' undertaken by the Chinese monk Huili in his "Biography of Xuanzang" (大唐大慈恩寺三藏法師傳 *Dà Táng dàcí 'ēnsì Sānzàng fǎshī zhuàn*, for a translation see Julien 1853; Beal 1914; Li 1959).

This work (VII century a.D.) is of great interest to both linguists and sinologists, as it offers significant attempts to describe sum subsets of Sanskrit grammar. Accounts on morphology of foreign languages are so rare in Pre-Modern China that contemporary linguistic analysis on Huili's work has been completely devoted to the interpretation of its morphological contents (see Van Gulik 1956; Brough 1973; Teng 2014). Much less attention has been paid to the Chinese transcriptions of Sanskrit terms, for instance the entire inflectional paradigm of the word *puruṣa* 'man' rendered in Chinese characters.

At that time the transcription systems used by the Chinese monks to transcribe Sanskrit words, mostly personal names and Buddhist terminology, were far from being homogeneous or standardized (Zürcher 1959). What is different here is that the original phonemic forms of the Sanskrit nominal endings are well-known, which makes it possible to use Huili's materials as a reference point for analyzing the phonology of Middle Chinese, which is otherwise known only from reconstructions.

Huili's choices in rendering Sanskrit nominal endings appear to be incoherent. The text freely alternates four different graphemes for the Sanskrit syllables *ṣa* and *ṣā* (namely, 殺, 沙, 鍛, and 廈). He even renders differently isomorphic elements, such as the theme *puruṣa-* and the terminations of the nominative singular, the dual dative and ablative, and the dual genitive and locative. Observing Pulleyblank's (1991) reconstruction of character pronunciation in Late Middle Chinese (LMC), Pulleyblank's forms display final consonants for characters employed by Huili for rendering open syllables in Sanskrit: this inconsistency is particularly evidente in the cases of 殺 and 鍛, both reconstructed as [ṣaːt] by Pulleyblank. Conversely, Huili adds the character 哆 (LMC [tʰá]) after 沙 (LMC [ṣa:]) specifically to represent the final dental of the ablative singular, which makes it unlikely that he had the segment [ṣa:t] at his disposal. This suggests that the forms reconstructed by Pulleyblank for LMC may be too conservative concerning the final consonant erosion that occurred in most modern Chinese dialects, including Mandarin.

Some other considerations can be made about the analysis of the *fǎnqiè* formulas. *Fǎnqiè* is a Chinese method of clarifying the phonetic realization of characters, which the reader might not have been familiar with. In several cases these indications appear crucial, as they suggest the reading of a missing character in the text, or make its pronunciation more similar to the reference Sanskrit syllable than Pulleyblank's (1991) reconstruction.

BIBLIOGRAPHY

Beal, S. 1914. *The Life of Hiuen-Tsiang by the Shaman Hwui Li*. London: Trübner.

Brough, J. 1973. "I-Ching on The Sanskrit Grammar", *Bulletin of the School of Oriental and African Studies* 36.2: 248–260.

Julien, S. 1853. *Histoire de La Vie de Hiouen-Thsang et de ses Voyages dans l'Inde, depuis l'an 629 jusqu'en 645, par Hoeï-Li et Yen-Thsong*. Paris: Impr. impériale.

Li, Y-H 1959. *The Life of Hsuan-Tsang, The Tripiṭaka-Master of the Great Tzu En Monastery, Compiled by the Monk Hui-Li*. Peking: The Chinese Buddhist Association.

Pulleyblank, E. G. 1991. *Lexicon of Reconstructed Pronunciation in Early Middle Chinese, Late Middle Chinese, and Early Mandarin*. Vancouver: UBC Press.

Teng, W-J. 2014. "Medieval Chinese Buddhist Exegesis and Chinese Grammatical Studies", *Táidà Fóxué yánjiū (Taiwan Journal of Buddhist Studies)* 28: 105–142.

Van Gulik, R. H. 1956. *Siddham: An Essay on the History of Sanskrit Studies in China and Japan*. Nagpur: International Academy of Indian Culture.

Zürcher E. 1959. *The Buddhist Conquest of China. The Spread and Adaptation of Buddhism in Early Medieval China*. Leiden: Brill.

SOURCES

CBETA, Vol. 50, n.2053 (大唐大慈恩寺三藏法師傳 *Dà Táng dàcí 'ēnsì Sānzàng fǎshī zhuàn*).

Rishi Rajpopat
The evolution of rule-conflict resolution tools
in the Pāṇinian grammatical tradition

I shall argue that contrary to the popular perception that the Pāṇinīyas, from Kātyāyana to Nāgeśa, broadly agree on how they define and resolve rule conflicts, the Pāṇinīyas actually had significantly different approaches to both conceptualizing and solving the problem of rule's conflict. I shall be using relevant material from the *Aṣṭādhyāyī*, Kātyāyana's *vārttika*s, the *Mahābhāṣya*, *Pradīpa* and *Udyota* (commentaries on the *Mahābhāṣya*), and from the *Paribhāṣenduśekhara* to make my case.

Using these sources, I shall attempt to reassemble the personalities and thought processes of these scholars, contemplate how they positioned themselves with respect to their predecessors, and also how and why they saw themselves donning one or more of the following hats: linguists, grammarians, commentators, peer-reviwers, philologists, Sanskritists etc.

Aleix Ruiz-Falqués
The *Mukhamattasāra*: a hidden Pali treasure

ABSTRACT

Around the 10th century CE, a scholar monk from Coḷa India or from Sri Lanka, named Vimalabuddhi (or Vajirabuddhi), composed the *Mukhamattadīpanī*, a detailed commentary on the grammar of Kaccāyana. This work, commonly known as *Nyāsa* ("The Support"), became particularly authoritative in Burma during the Pagan Period. It is not an exaggeration to say that Vimalabuddhi's commentary achieved a para-canonical status over the centuries. It influenced a great number of grammatical and non-grammatical Pali works in Burma. Perhaps one of the most conspicous testimonies of this influence is the *Mukhamattasāra* ("Essence of the *Mukhamattadīpanī*"), a summary of the *Mukhamattadīpanī* in one thousand stanzas.

The title *Mukhamattasāra* is well-known from listings in manuscript archives, authoritative chronicles, catalogues and medieval inscriptions of library donations. The authorship is ascribed to a certain Sāgara or Guṇasāgara of Pagan (Burma). Although the title is well recorded, the text itself has never been edited and it seems that no modern scholar has examined it directly. In this presentation I am going to discuss the contents of the work and how the editio princeps is being prepared. I will also touch on its historical significance and how it helps us to understand the role of *vyākaraṇa* in the Theravada tradition of Burma and Southeast Asia.

Małgorzata Sulich-Cowley
Do we or do we not have negative compounds in Sanskrit?

INTRODUCTION

This presentation aims to discuss the potential cross-linguistic relevance of Sanskrit negative compounds. There is no unanimity among scholars on the issue of compounding and, further, types of compounds. Compounds are not easily definable even in one language due to the problems with determining the category of a word, crucial element of a compound (Bauer 2017: 3). The problem of the basic, or universal, definition becomes even greater when we aim at comparing compounding across various languages, or try to apply the tools devised in one linguistic tradition to another. To a large extent modern classifications of compounds refer to Sanskrit terminology and while they do borrow the rough concepts from Sanskrit grammarians, they tend to modify them to suit their needs. When we look at various categories proposed by different scholars (Bloomfield 1933; Bally 1950; Marchand 1969; Spencer 1991; Fabb 1998; Olsen 2001; Haspelmath 2002; Bauer 2001; Booij 2005), we see that they are based on varied criteria. Pāṇini's division into *dvandvas*, *tatpuruṣas* and *bahuvrīhi*s has been employed in various ways in different approaches, significantly deviating from the original meaning of these terms. Interestingly, all such classifications omit the category of *avyayībhāvas*. To what extent then can the classification proposed by Western scholars be considered universal if they are based on the classification created for a particular language? This lack of universality would, in turn, make them inapplicable for comparative purposes. Haspelmath (2012; 2018) might be right when he says that in most of the cases linguists do not compare languages but they merely describe one language with the help of categories created for another.

SHIFT BETWEEN TRADITIONS

The case of compounds is a prime example of how we shift between the two respective traditions while describing linguistic phenomena. I would like to discuss the issue of mutual discrepancy in Sanskrit and Western linguistics from the point of view of negative compounds in Sanskrit, as they are an excellent case of such constant shifting. The fundamental difference between Sanskrit and other linguistic tradition in the West is the ability to conceive the category of the *negative compound*. This is possible due to Pāṇini's approach to negation. In the *Aṣṭādhyāyī* the particle *nañ* (the main negative particle) stands for both the sentential particle *na* and the "privative" prefix *a-/an-*. Whether we see expressions such as *na pacati* 'does not cook' or *abrāhmaṇa* 'a non-Brahmin', in both case we deal with a particle that stems from the common term *nañ*. In other words, *nañ* represents both a particle and a prefix in modern linguistic terms. It is precisely this distinction (or, perhaps, the lack of distinction between two expressions of negation) that allows for the existence of the negative compounds in Sanskrit. The condition for a compound to take place is for both (or more) elements in it to be termed *pada* befor the composition takes place. A prefix cannot be assigned such a designation, while a particle can; the entire class of *avyayībhāva*s is built on this.

This is the first level of discrepancy between the two traditions that can be observed. While "alpha privative" formations are not unique to Sanskrit and can be found across Indo-European languages. Usually they are not treated as compounds. This leads us to the second discrepancy problem — types of compounds.

Pāṇini's approach to *nañsamāsa*s is clearly morphological; he treats them as *tatpuruṣa* compounds where their gender and number are determined by the last member, and where the first element serves as a qualifier. Pāṇini's criteria for such a classification underwent, however, some changes in the hand of later commentator, starting with Patañjali who placed the emphasis on the semantic predominance of one of the members in a compound. As negative compounds are a very particular case from both the point of view of the general notion of absence or non-existence, and from that of the pragmatic perspective of how they are actually used, it seems that Pāṇini's description is not sufficient. Negative compounds can, albeit not always, be interpreted through the lens of non-existence qualifying some existence; but they can also possess an entirely external referent. This potential exocentricity is problematic for Sanskrit grammarians who operate between the options of *tatpuruṣa* and *bahuvrīhi*, and are bound by Pāṇini's categorisation of the former. While they do acknowledge that negative compounds possess an external referent, they do not consider this feature crucial enough to make them become inherently *bahuvrīhi*s.

If we operate within the Pāṇinian system, we are left with no choice but to accept *nañsamāsa*s as *tatpuruṣa*s, although of a special kind. At the same time, the classification of compounds proposed in the West by Scalise and Bisetto (2005) allowing for exocentricity in each of the proposed type of compounds can easily accommodate Sanskrit constructions such as *abrāhmaṇa*.

Finally, we have to deal with the incompatibility of two negation types, namely: *prasajyapratiṣedha* 'negation (subsequent to tentatively) applying' and *paryudāsapratiṣedha* 'limitational negation'. This division does not neatly correspond to sentential versus term negation in that negative compounds can exhibit both types depending on their required interpretation. In other words, *nañ* in a compound «can be construed with the nominal following it in the compound, or it can be construed with a verb» (Cardona 1967: 34). In the former case (*paryudāsa*), the meaning of the particle *nañ* would be that of *bheda* 'difference', which we could observe in the example of *abrāhmaṇa*; while in the latter (*prasajya*), it is the meaning of *abhāva* 'absence' as it requires the provisional acceptance of an operation, which is subsequently denied.

DISCREPANCIES, DISCREPANCIES

The terminological discrepancy regarding negative compounds can be therefore discussed on various levels. Firstly, there is the issue of introducing the concept of a negative compound, which is not common (or even accepted) in Western linguistics. Secondly, there arises the problem with the exocentricity of such compounds and their potential classification as *bahuvrīhi samāsas*. Finally, there is the issue of the type of negation such a compound exhibits, whether we are dealing with *prasajya* or *paryudāsapratiṣedha*.

All these three issues can be discussed within the Sanskrit grammatical tradition, where they are not free from contradictions and various interpretations. Yet any attempt to analyse *nañsamāsas* in comparative perspective with respect to similar expression in other languages (even within the Indo-European family) reveals the lack of common comparative criteria. If, as Haspelmath claims, most word classes are language specific and universality of linguistic categories is a myth, no comparative study becomes possible. If it is impossible to apply word-classes cross-linguistically, how is it possible to define cross-linguistically what a compound is? What criteria would we have to devise to include *abrāhmaṇa* or *aneka* into the domain of compounds in Western linguistics? Can we treat them as compounds based on Sanskrit grammar and still try to categorise them based on Western patterns? Are we bound to describe one language in terms of theories devised for that particular language only?

Pāṇinian system has been an inspiration for modern Western linguistics for decades and historical linguistics has drawn from Sanskrit for much longer. Despite Sanskrit being an Indo-European language and thus sharing numerous features with languages such as Latin and Greek, we can notice certain systematic discrepancies between the two linguistic descriptions. The manner in which word classes are defined by respective linguistic traditions is by no means uniform.

REFERENCES

Bally, C. 1944[2]. *Linguistique générale et linguistique francaise*. Berne: A. Francke.

Bauer, L. 2017. *Compounds and Compounding*. Oxford: Oxford University Press.

Bisetto A., and S. Scalise. 2005. "The classification of compounds", *Lingue e Linguaggio* IV.2: 319–332.

Bloomfield, L. 1933. *Language*. New York: Holt.

Booij, G. 2005. *The Grammar of Words*. Oxford: Oxford University Press.

Cardona, G. 1967. "Negations in Pāṇinian rules", *Language* 43.1: 34–56.

Cartoni, B., and M.-A. Lefer. 2011. "Negation and lexical morphology across languages: Insights from a trilingual translation corpus", *Poznań Studies in Contemporary Linguistics* 47.4: 795–843.

Fabb, N. 1998. "Compounding", in A. Spencer & A. M. Zwicky (eds.), *The Handbook of Morphology*, 66–83. Oxford: Blackwell.

Haspelmath, M. 2012. "How to compare major word-classes across the world's languages", *UCLA Working Papers in Linguistics, Theories of Everything* 17: 109–113.

Haspelmath, M. 2018. "How comparative concepts and descriptive linguistic categories are different", in D. van Olmen, T. Mortelmans & F. Brisard (eds.), *Aspects of Linguistic Variation*, 83–113. Berlin: De Gruyter.

Haspelmath M., and A. Sims. 2010. *Understanding Morphology*. London: Hodder Education Hachette UK.

Joshi, S. 2012. "Affixal negation — direct, indirect and their subtypes", *Revue Syntaxe et Sémantique* 13: 49–63.

Joshi, S. 2020. "Affixal negation", in V. Déprez & M. T. Espinal (eds.), *The Oxford handbook of negation*, 75–89. Oxford: Oxford University Press.

Marchand, M. 1969[2]. *The categories and types of present-day English word-formation*. München: Verlag C. H. Beck.

Olsen, S. 2001. "Copulative Compounds. A Closer Look at the Interface Between Morphology and Syntax", in G. Booij & J. van Marle (eds.), *Yearbook of Morphology 2000*, 279–320. Berlin: Springer.

Scalise, S., and A. Fábregas. 2010. "The head in compounding", in S. Scalise & I. Vogel (eds.), *Cross-disciplinary issues in compounding*, pp. 109–126. Amsterdam: Benjamins.

Spencer, A. 1991. *Morphological Theory*. Oxford: Blackwell.

Mittal Trivedi
Exploring the foundation of the *lakāra* in the *tiṅanta* section of the *Vaiyākaraṇasiddhāntakaumudī* and the *Prakriyākaumudī*

ABSTRACT

Bhaṭṭoji Dīkṣita is known as the pioneer of the Navya Vyākaraṇa school due to the *Vaiyākaraṇasiddhāntakaumudī*'s (SK) *prakriyā*-based approach to the grammar of Pāṇini. Not many sources note, however, its surprising resemblance with the *Prakriyākaumudī* of Rāmacandra Śeṣa, a fact that I believe is significant for understanding the development of the SK as the voice of Pāṇinian grammar in the age of *Navya Vyākaraṇa*.

Tradition touts the idea that Dīkṣita is responsible for bringing the grammatical tradition back to its Pāṇinian roots through his seminal work, but a verbatim comparison with his textual predecessor shows structural incongruities which argue that the *Prakriyākaumudī*'s approach was a little more logical for the purposes of a derivational grammar. For example:

- Dīkṣita assumes what is traditionally claimed to be the Pāṇinian style of explanation and introduces the *pratyaya* first, leaving the utilization of the *dhātu* to the auspices of the reader's contemplation. In contrast to this, Rāmacandra begins the verbal section by presenting the structure of the derivation as a juxtaposition between *prakṛti* and *pratyaya*.
- While Dīkṣita introduces the rule *dhātoḥ* A. 3.1.91 in the *kṛdanta* section to emphasize its use in the development of a nominal form, Rāmacandra has situated it in the *tiṅanta* section instead, in line with his presentation of the *prakṛti* and *pratyaya*.

Additionally, certain indications in the text of the *Vaiyākaraṇasiddhāntakaumudī* provide evidence for the idea that Dīkṣita's text may indeed be a commentary like many scholars believe today. Pāṇini utilizes the *lakāra* mechanism to facilitate the derivation of verbal forms using the ten tenses/modes provided from the *adhikāra bhūte* (A. 3.2.84) up to the rule *mati-buddhi-pūjanārthebhyaś ca* (A. 3.2.188). Similarities in *prakriyā* are introduced when these rules apply after a *dhātu* through *utsarga/apavāda* to *tiṅanta* or *kṛdanta* forms essentially governed by the rules *dhātoḥ* (A. 3.1.91), *vartamāne laṭ* (A. 3.2.123), *laḥ karmaṇi ca bhāve cā akarmakebhyaḥ* (A. 3.4.69), *lasya* (A. 3.4.77), and *tip-tas-jhi...* (A. 3.4.78). Ultimately, these rules have been engineered into a tangential structure by the *prakriyā* school as the conceptual juxtaposition of the rules *dhātoḥ* (A. 3.1.91) and *kṛd atiṅ* (A. 3.1.93) is disrupted.

Despite this disruption, it is essential to understand the attempt made by Rāmacandra and Dīkṣita to simplify grammatical studies in their time. To understand one facet of this, I will compare the development of the concept of the *lakāra* between the two texts to assess innovation, structural integrity, and cohesiveness using the initial four *sūtra*s of the *tiṅanta* section in each text as my subject of inquiry.

My assessment also includes a study of the *Prasāda* and *Tattvabodhinī* commentaries of Viṭṭhala and Jñānendra Sarasvati to understand the dissemination of the *mūla* text. This study consists of a small part of my ongoing PhD thesis, wherein I am attempting to explore the extent to which the *prakriyā* school is faithful to the structure of Pāṇini's grammar and the subsequent comprehension of grammatical concepts. While the *prakriyā* school has undoubtedly contributed to a more simplified view of Pāṇinian grammar, the question remains as to whether it facilitates the holistic understanding of Sanskrit grammar that can be obtained through studying the *Aṣṭādhyāyī*.

AṢṬĀDHYĀYĪ

(1)   [*dhātoḥ* A 3.1.91] [*paras ca* A 3.1.2] *vartamāne laṭ* [*pratyayaḥ* A 3.1.1] [*ādyudāttaś ca* A 3.1.3]
"The substitute of the affix [*pratyaya* A. 3.1.1] *laṭ* with an *udātta* accent on the initial syllable [*ādyudātta* A. 3.1.3] applies after [*para* A. 3.1.2] a verbal base [*dhātu* A. 3.1.91] when the present tense [*vartamāne*] has to be signified" (*Aṣṭādhyāyī* 3.2.123).

(2)   [*dhātoḥ* A. 3.1.91] [*paras* ca A. 3.1.2] *laḥ* [*kartari* A. 3.4.67] *karmaṇi ca bhāve cākarmakebhyaḥ* [*ādyudāttaś ca* A. 3.1.3]
"An *l*-form (*laḥ*), with an *udātta* accent on the initial syllable [*ādyudātta*], applies after [*para* A. 3.1.2] a verbal base [*dhatu* 3.1.91] when an agent [*kartṛ* A. 3.4.67] as well as a patient [*karman*] has to be signified (for *sakarmaka*), and when an agent [*kartṛ*] or the mere action [*bhāva*] has to be signified, but only when an objectless [*akarmaka*] verbal base is used" (*Aṣṭādhyāyī* 3.4.69).

(3) *lasya*
"[The following affixes are substituted] in the place of *l*-forms [*lasya*]"
(*Aṣṭādhyāyī* 3.4.77).

(4) [*dhātoḥ* A. 3.1.91] [*paraś ca* A. 3.1.2] *tip-tas-jhi-sip-thas-tha-mib-vas-mas-ta-ātāṃ-jha-thās-āthāṃ-dhvam-iḍ-vahi-mahiṅ* [*pratyayaḥ* A. 3.1.1] [*ādyudāttaś ca* A. 3.1.3] [*anudāttau sup-pitau* A. 3.1.4]
"The affixes *tip-tas-jhi-sip-thas-tha-mib-vas-mas-ta-tam-jha-thās-āthāṃ-dhvam-iḍ-vahi-mahiṅ* apply after [*paraś ca* A. 3.1.2] a verbal base [*dhatoḥ* A. 3.1.91] in the place of the *lakāra* and are high pitched on the initial syllable [*ādyudāttaś ca* 3.1.3] with the exception of the affixes with a P-marker [*sup pitau* A. 3.1.4] which are *anudātta*-pitched accent [*anudāttau* A. 3.1.4] (*Aṣṭādhyāyī* 3.4.78).

(5) *dhātoḥ* || 3.1.91|| *ā tṛtīyādhyāyāntaṃ vakṣyamāṇāḥ pratyayā dhātor jñeyāḥ. teṣv ādau daśa lakārāḥ pradarśyante: laṭ, liṭ, luṭ, lṛṭ, leṭ, loṭ, laṅ, liṅ, luṅ, lṛṅ.*
"The affixes which are presented until the end of the third book are known to be attached after verbal bases. Of (these affixes) the ten *l*-forms will be presented".

(6) *laḥ karmaṇi ca bhāve cā karmakebhyaḥ* || 3.4.69 || *lukārāḥ sakarmakād dhātoḥ karmaṇi kartari cā karmakād bhāve kartari ca syuḥ. 'pratyayaḥ' 'paraś ca' ity anuvartate.*
"*l*-forms apply to transitive verbal bases (A. 3.1.91) when an agent (*kartṛ*) or a patient (*karman*) is signified and to intransitive verbal bases when an agent or the mere action is signified. (The rules) '*pratyayaḥ*' (A. 3.1.1) and '*paraś ca*' (A. 3.1.2) are carried over here".

(7) *vartamāne laṭ* || 3.2.123 || *ārabdh āparisamāpta-kriyopalakṣite kāle vācye dhātor laṭ pratyayaḥ syāt. aṭāvitau. ādeśavidhānasāmarthyān na lasy etasaṃjñā.*
"The *l*-form *laṭ* should be applied after a verbal base when as a tense whose action is described from its inception to its end. '*a*' and '*Ṭ*' are markers. To justify the execution of a substitute the (remaining) '*l*' is not designated a marker".

(8) *lasya* || 3.4.77 || *ityadhikṛtya.*
"Within the domain of this rule... (the next rule will apply)".

(9) *vartamāne laṭ* || 3.2.123 || *vartamāna kriyāvṛtter dhātor laṭ syāt. aṭāvitau.*
"The affix *laṭ* should apply after a verbal base (3.1.91) when an action (*kriyā*) is signified (*kriyāvṛtter*) in the present tense (*vartamāna*). 'a' and 'ṭ' are markers".

(10) *laḥ karmaṇi ca bhāve cā karmakebhyaḥ* || 3.4.69 || *lakārāḥ sakarmakebhyaḥ karmaṇi kartari ca syur akarmakebhyo bhāve kartari ca.*
"Verbal affixes should apply after transitive verbal bases (A. 3.1.91) when an agent (*kartṛ*) or a patient (*karman*) has to be signified and after intransitive verbal bases when an agent or the mere action has to be signified".

(11) *lasya* || 3.4.77 || *adhikāro 'yam.*
"This is a heading rule [valid until the end of the fifth book]".

(12) *tip-tas-jhi...* || 3.4.78 || *ete 'ṣṭādaśa lādeśāḥ syuḥ.*
"These [*tip-tas-jhi...*] eighteen [suffixes] should be the substitutes for the primary verbal affixes [*lādeśa*]".

PRIMARY SOURCES

Trivedi, R. B. K. P., and A. K. Trivedi (eds.). 1931. *Prakriyākaumudī of Rāmacandra (In Two Parts). Part II.* Poona: Bhandarkar Oriental Research Institute.

Paṇsikar, V. L. S. (ed.). 1908. *The Siddhāntakaumudī with Tattvabodhinī Commentary of Jnanendra Sarasvati and Subodhinī Commentary of Jayakrishna.* Bombay: Nirnayasāgar Press.

REFERENCES

Bali, S. 1976. *Bhaṭṭoji Dīkṣita: his Contribution to Sanskrit Grammar.* New Delhi: Munshiram Manoharlal Publishers.

Candotti, M. P. 2012a. "The Role and Import of the Metalinguistic Chapters in the 'New' Pāṇinian Grammars", in *Saṃskṛta-Sādhutā. Studies in Honor of Professor Ashok Aklujkar.* New Delhi: D. K. Printworld.

Candotti, M. P. 2012b. "Traditional Stocks of Examples and Their Influence on the First Prakriyā Grammars", in *Studies in Sanskrit Grammars. Proceedings of the Vyākaraṇa Section of the 14th World Sanskrit Conference.*

Deshpande, M. 2002. "Fluidity of Early Grammatical Categories in Sanskrit", *Journal of the American Oriental Society* 122.2: 244–47.

Deshpande, M. 1998. "Evolution of the Notion of Authority (*Prāmāṇya*) in the Pāṇinian Tradition", *Histoire Épistémologie Langage* 20: 5–28.

Deshpande, M. 1987. "Pāṇinian syntax and the changing notion of sentence", *Annals of the Bhandarkar Oriental Research Institute* 68: 55–98.